# The Complete Guide to Rat Training

# Debbie Ducommun

ESTES VALLEY
LIBRARY

*The Complete Guide to Rat Training*
Debbie Ducommun

Project Team
Editor: Mary E. Grangeia
Copy Editor: Stephanie Fornino
Designer: Angela Stanford
Indexer: Ann W. Truesdale

TFH Publications®
President/CEO: Glen S. Axelrod
Executive Vice President: Mark E. Johnson
Editor-in-Chief: Albert Connelly, Jr.
Production Manager: Kathy Bontz

TFH Publications, Inc.®
One TFH Plaza
Third and Union Avenues
Neptune City, NJ 07753

Printed and bound in China
18 19 20 21 22   7 9 11 10 8

**Library of Congress Cataloging-in-Publication Data**
Ducommun, Debbie, 1958-
    The complete guide to rat training : tricks and games for rat fun and fitness / Debbie Ducommun.
        p. cm.
    Includes index.
    ISBN 978-0-7938-0651-5 (alk. paper)
    1. Rats--Training. 2. Rats as pets. I. Title.
    SF459.R3D83 2008
    636.935'2--dc22
                        2008014979

The Leader In Responsible Animal Care For Over 50 Years!®
www.tfh.com

# Table of Contents

# Introduction

I got my first pet rat when I was about ten years old. He was my buddy, and he would ride around on my shoulder. As a teenager, I had a whole family of rats and spent many happy hours teaching them tricks. I still have a home movie showing my pet rats jumping from the top of their cage to my shoulder and back again.

Rats are very much like little dogs, except I think that they are more like people. Pet rats love nothing better than to spend time with their humans. Teaching them tricks and games is a wonderful way to interact with them. The more time you spend with your rats, the more they will want to be with you, and the easier it will be to train them. I wish you lots of happy times with your own pet rats.

# Chapter 1
# Rats and Humans

**M**any people are amazed that rats can be kept as pets, let alone that they can be trained. Yet long ago, rats found it advantageous to live with people. They could manage more comfortably in farmlands and cities than in the wild.

Despite the fact that rats have for the most part peacefully cohabitated with humans since the Stone Age, it is sad that they were first domesticated in England and France during the 1800s solely for use as lures in the inhumane "sport" of rat baiting. The object of this so-called entertainment was to put a dog into a pit (a small arena) with a large number of rats to see how many he could kill. Bets were taken on how long it took to accomplish this ghastly task. Because of the popularity of these gambling events, thousands of wild rats were captured and sent to their eventual demise in ratting contests.

Rat baiting was finally abolished, but unfortunately, this cruel blood sport flourished for nearly 70 years. During that time, many wild rats were corralled, and it was noticed that a few of them were found to have unusual coat color mutations such as all black or albino (all white with pink eyes). The rat catchers saved some of these rarer individuals out of curiosity and proceeded to breed them for their unique qualities.

Scientists later discovered that the mutated gene that produced a solid-colored coat (such as black) also affected behavior and temperament because these rats were more docile than the common brown-ticked rat. It appeared that not only were solid-colored rats distinctive because of their appearance, they were also unusually tame.

Once it was discovered that these rats made good pets, they were bred specifically for that purpose. Rats became extremely popular companion animals for little girls during the Victorian era (1839–1901). Evidence for this can be seen in photographs from the period, which show the children posing in their best clothes with their pet rats sitting happily in their laps. As a girl, well-known author Beatrix Potter (1866–1943), who was famous for her beautifully illustrated children's books, had a pet rat named Sammy, who later appeared in some of her stories.

In the early 1900s, scientists recognized how similar rats were to humans and regularly began breeding them for use as laboratory animals. But domestic rats were pets first and laboratory animals second. Recently, rats have seen a resurgence in popularity as family pets and have even been immortalized as lovable characters in movies like *Ratatouille*.

**Domesticated rats have been changed from their wild ancestors through a long process of selective breeding.**

# DOMESTICATED VERSUS WILD AND FERAL ANIMALS

As is the case with the rat, numerous species of creatures have been domesticated for thousands of generations, yet people tend to be confused about the differences among wild, domesticated, and feral animals. Knowing what distinguishes them from each other can help you better understand why socialized animals make better pets for a variety of reasons.

## Wild Animals

There are many physical and behavioral differences between a domesticated animal and his wild ancestor. Wild animals are more aggressive and defensive. They are suspicious and scared of anything unfamiliar and will explore things in their environment very cautiously. They tend to be nervous and flighty, especially if they are members of a species that is preyed upon often. These reflexes and instincts are necessary for them to survive in the wild.

Nevertheless, some wild animals can be tamed if you are able to spend the time necessary to help them adapt to their human family. Taming is really a form of socialization: A tamed wild animal has become accustomed to being with humans and has therefore lost most of his fear of them. However, because he is still a wild creature, he will retain his instinctual fear of the unknown and can react unpredictably and aggressively in untried situations.

### Domesticated Animals

Although a common misconception, domesticated animals are not simply *tamed* wild animals. They have been changed from their wild ancestors through a long process of selective breeding. Only the individuals with the best qualities were chosen for reproduction. Eventually, after subsequent generations, most of the wild tendencies were bred out.

Changes in temperament were a direct consequence of the many physical changes brought on by selective breeding. For example, domesticated animals became much less aggressive and fearful because their adrenal glands, which are responsible for producing adrenaline (the "fight or flight" hormone), became less necessary and grew smaller. As a result, domesticated animals are more docile and calm in unfamiliar surroundings than their wild cousins. Rather than immediately running away from the unexpected, they tend to be very curious about unfamiliar objects or creatures in their environment and will approach them much more readily. As long as they have been well socialized by humans, they see new individuals as an opportunity to make a friend rather than as a threat to attack.

### Feral Animals

Feral animals are domesticated animals who have not received human socialization because they were born of parents who escaped into the wild and now live there. Because they were not exposed to humans as youngsters, they do not recognize them as part of their social group and react to them with fear. However, most feral animals, especially communal species, can be successfully socialized to humans with time and patience.

### THE SOCIAL RAT

Domestic rats have become popular pets because they are extremely social animals. They prefer to live in family groups and have a natural tendency to form strong bonds with other individuals. This is one reason why rats are

## Wild Colors

The normal wild rat color is called agouti, after a South American rodent with fur of the same color. In an agouti coat, each hair is banded with three colors: gray at the bottom, brown in the middle, and black at the tip. From a distance, the overall impression is usually a medium brown, but the agouti coat is quite variable, and different individuals can appear dark brown, brownish-gray, or even quite red. Many species of wild rodents have an agouti coat.

fairly easy to train. They want to please their family members.

Each individual learns which species to accept as part of his family through socialization. Socialization occurs through contact and interaction. When domestic rats are socialized to humans as babies, they form strong bonds with them. Even puppies and kittens must be socialized by humans to become good pets. If they do not receive early human interaction, they will become feral animals who are frightened of people.

Likewise, because rats are social species by nature, it is imperative that they have regular contact with other individuals. It is abnormal for a rat to live alone, and a single pet rat will be lonely and bored unless he gets plenty of attention from his owner. Lack of contact with other rats or humans can also cause him to become neurotic, withdrawn, anxious, and even aggressive.

**Rats are very social animals who need daily interaction with other individuals, ideally with other rats as well as their humans.**

## Rats as Pets

When shopping for your small pet, you may be told that single rats will do fine and that they will bond more strongly to humans. There is some truth to these statements, but they don't tell the whole story.

While a single rat will crave human attention and be extremely devoted, this is mostly because you are his only source of social interaction. It's my belief that a single pet rat should be given the opportunity to interact with humans for at least four hours a day. If you can't give your pet sufficient daily attention, it is unfair to keep him alone. A rat who lives with other rats will still be eager to interact with humans as long as he has been regularly handled. The more human attention a rat gets, the more he will desire it.

It is always worth the trouble to make sure that all pet rats have their social needs met. If you want to train your rats to do tricks, they must spend as much time with you as possible. The best trick performers are self-confident, outgoing, friendly rats, and they will only be this way with a satisfying social life.

## Similarities Between Humans and Rats

Rats have always been a source of fascination to humans, which may be one reason they were eventually kept as house pets. Highly intelligent and resourceful, they make great companions and are certainly fun to watch. It is amazing how alike humans and rats are in the way we communicate and live, and these similarities may explain the deep bond that humans have developed with these charming and entertaining creatures.

I think that rats are more like humans than any other domestic pet. We are both highly adaptable generalists, which means that we are good at many different things, unlike animals who have highly specialized skills and lifestyles. We have similar physiologies and nervous systems, and like humans, rats have hands that can manipulate objects. We have similar social needs and diets, and we even both react the same way to almost all medications. In fact, according to studies done at the National Human Genome Research Institute (NHGRI), our genetic code is more like that of rats than of dogs or cats.

Rats are also surprisingly self-aware and have distinct personalities. They use similar forms of communication and display the same types of emotions that we do. They're companionable, curious, and enjoy being touched. They dream as we dream and can even have such a strong desire for food that they will indulge themselves to obesity. Rats will even laugh when you tickle them!

I have heard numerous anecdotes demonstrating that rats can show a range of feelings: compassion, bravery, sympathy, hope, devotion, grief, anxiety, greed, jealousy, vanity, and pride. One of my favorite stories is about a friend's rat named Max, who clearly showed pride in a special possession. One Sunday afternoon, Pat was sitting on her living room floor working on a large painting. She had a cup of coffee and a box of cookies beside her. Her white rat Max came by for a visit and became very excited at the sight of the big box of

# Adopting Rats

You can obtain rats from sources other than a pet shop. In some areas, you can find hobby breeders who produce quality rats. Homeless rats are occasionally available at animal shelters (large shelters in California almost always have rats up for adoption), and there are rat rescue groups in certain parts of the country. Rescue groups often take in unwanted litters of babies who have been well socialized. You will find a list of rat breeders and rat rescues on the Internet at www.ratfanclub.org.

One of the similarities between rats and humans is their ability to manipulate objects with their hands.

treats. She said, "Go ahead and take a cookie, Max." So Max took the cookie and left with it. A few days later, Pat was entertaining some visitors. They were sitting in the living room talking when suddenly Max appeared, holding his cookie high over his head as he proudly entered the room with a parade gait. He glowingly passed in front of each and every person to show off his treasure, a whole cookie! Everyone was completely charmed by him.

Rats display strong family bonds, too. Those who live together tend to take care of one another and show concern when a family member is ill or injured. Domestic rats will sometimes bring food to an individual who isn't coming out to eat. They may also show compassion in other ways. Charlie, a rat who lived with Arlene Thompson in Stafford, Virginia, suffered from frequent seizures. If he was in the company of his brothers when he had a convulsion, his brother Donavan would climb up on his back and try to hold him down! Rosalie Elliott, who lived in Pembroke Pines, Florida, let her female rats live free in their own room. (They were all litter box trained.) One day while the Elliotts were away from home, one of the rats, Sandy, got her foot caught when the lid of a wooden nesting box fell on top of it. When Rosalie's husband returned home, he heard a commotion coming from the rats' room. Sandy was screaming and the other rats were frantically chewing at the lid trying to free her leg. Pebbles, Sandy's mother, was trying to comfort her in vain and was getting bitten for her troubles. Rosalie's husband felt compelled to rescue Sandy, the first time he had ever touched any of the rats. After witnessing their concern and the way they all tried to help each other, he had a newfound respect for them.

Rats can even be heroes. The April 14, 1998, issue of *The Mirror*, a British newspaper, ran the story of Fido, a rat who saved his humans from a fire. An electric heater started a blaze in their home at 2 am. Fido pushed his way out of his cage, jumped onto the burning carpet, and ran past the flames, climbing 15 stairs to scratch on the bedroom door of nine-year-old Shannon, who then woke her mother, Lisa Gumbley. The whole family was able to escape unharmed. Meanwhile, the family's German Shepherd had remained asleep at the end of Lisa's bed. Fido was rewarded for saving his family's lives with his favorite foods.

## UNDERSTANDING YOUR RATS

Understanding your pet is the best way to develop a strong relationship, build trust, and form a lifelong bond. In fact, the best trainers are excellent observers of animal behavior. The better you understand an animal, the better you can train him. So for you to really know what your rat is trying to communicate to you, you'll need to pay close attention to his vocalizations and body language.

### Vocalizations

The normal rat vocalizations that humans can hear are mostly squeaks that express annoyance, dislike, pain, or fear. The louder and higher pitched the squeak, the more afraid or hurt the rat may be. A rat who is agitated or anxious may grind his teeth together quickly, creating a vigorous rasping or chittering noise. This is a warning to back off. Rats who are defending their territory can sometimes make an explosive puffing sound and can even hiss somewhat like a defensive cat. These sounds are rare, though.

At certain times, an individual will actually learn to make noises to communicate with a human. These can take the form of a soft squeaking or high-pitched grunting. A rat who learns to make sounds like this is probably trying to say "You're my friend. I like being with you." However, care must be taken to distinguish these learned sounds from wheezing noises caused by

# Grooming Customs

Rubbing a rat on his cheek will often stimulate an interesting reflex that causes him to extend his arm and fingers on that side. When a rat is feeling relaxed, scratching him behind the shoulder blades will usually stimulate him to groom you back if you offer your other hand. A rat will usually groom you with soft licks and sometimes nibbles. If your rat nibbles or nips too hard, squeak as if you are a rat being hurt and he will learn to be more gentle.

respiratory disease because they can sound similar. Wheezing always occurs in time with breathing, and although it can occur on and off, it's usually heard when the rat is going about his normal business or even when he is asleep.

Sounds a rat makes to communicate will usually occur only when a person is nearby or holding and talking to the rat. For example, when a rat is contented and relaxed—often when he is being petted—he can engage in a behavior called bruxing. This produces a slow grinding noise, almost a crunching sound. Bruxing is the equivalent of purring. It can be accompanied by another behavior called eye popping. This occurs when the rat flexes muscles that run alongside the eyes, causing the eyeball to quickly move in and out of the sockets. Although this behavior can be alarming at first, be reassured that a rat doing eye pops is as happy as he can be.

## Body Language

Rats also communicate with each other through scent, touch, and body language. They have a universal set of body movements and behaviors that is quite diverse. Learning this body language is a great way to get inside your rat's mind and understand his thoughts, moods, and needs. You will begin to recognize that many of the unusual behaviors your rat displays have a lot to do with his senses and the way in which he interprets and navigates his environment.

Of all their senses, vision is the weakest. Nevertheless, rats still

**Rats communicate with each other through scent, touch, and body language. Learning this body language is a great way to get inside your rat's mind and understand his thoughts, moods, and needs.**

# LAUGHING RATS

In 1998, psychologist Jaak Panksepp, Ph.D., discovered that rats laugh in ultrasound. While Panksepp was studying the biological origins of joy at the Medical College of Ohio at Toledo, one of his graduate students came up with the idea of listening to rat vocalizations with a bat detector, an instrument that lowers ultrasounds so that they are audible to humans. The study group turned the bat detector on, began tickling rats, and found that they were chirping vigorously in ultrasound. "It sounded like a children's playground," said Panksepp.

Although other scientists are skeptical, Panksepp believes that the rats' ultrasonic chirps are laughter because the sounds occur in the same situations that laughter occurs in humans. The rats laugh when playing and wrestling together and when tickled by humans. They laugh the most when tickled at the nape of the neck. They also chirp when anticipating a treat—just imagine children laughing happily when told they can have a cookie! Young rats laugh more than older rats, just as children laugh more than adult humans. The rats appeared to enjoy being tickled during the testing and would seek out a human hand to be tickled. They formed a preference for hands that tickled them rather than hands that just petted them. Those rats who chirped the most were also the ones who wrestled most vigorously with a human hand and directed the most play bites to the hand. Likewise, giggling to rats puts them in a playful mood!

**If you want to train your rat to do tricks, he should spend as much time with you as possible.**

communicate with visual signals. A rat will indicate submission by lowering his ears and dominant aggression by arching his back and bristling his fur. Other rats know when a rat sees something interesting by his erect ears pointing toward the object of interest. A rat who sees something scary, like a snake, can wiggle his tail as a warning to other rats.

Rats are nearsighted and can probably see details only a few feet (a meter) away. But they see movement extremely well—even at a distance—and can see in very dim light. They are mostly—but not entirely—color blind. Some domestic rats, especially those with pink eyes, have a tendency to sit and sway, weaving their head from side to side. This behavior improves depth perception and helps the rat focus on stationary objects. It occurs in rats with poor eyesight as well.

Many of the rat's other senses are acute, however. For example, they have a keen sense of hearing. They can recognize and locate noises to within half a foot (15.2 cm). They also have an excellent sense of smell, which helps them locate food, along with a highly developed sense of taste that helps them know what is safe to eat. You have probably seen your rat stand up and wave his face into the air. This is because he gathers information about his environment from a combination of scents and sounds. When your rat grabs your hands, he is probably enthralled by the smell of another rat on your skin.

Another form of communication related to smell is scent marking. A rat will sometimes mark another rat—or a human—as part of his social group by climbing over him and marking him with urine. Some rats will also urine mark objects they walk over as part of their territory. Dominant rats, especially dominant males, are more likely to urine mark than other rats. When your rat rubs his sides along objects or rubs his hands on the ground, he is scent marking, as well as making a visual territorial gesture.

Rats are also highly sensitive to touch. They can use their whiskers to help them sense their environment when they are wandering about in the dark. They see being petted by a human as a form of social grooming. If you want to pet your rat and he doesn't want you to, it may be because he isn't in the mood. Rats mostly like to be groomed when they are relaxed and sleepy. Some are more comfortable being petted if they can hide inside something like a box or underneath a blanket. Each rat will have a favorite spot to be petted. Common favorites are the shoulders, the top of the head, and the cheeks. If your rat licks or nibbles your hands, face, or skin, he is displaying grooming behavior toward you. Because he sees you as part of his group, he feels moved to reciprocate.

All these behaviors help rats to survive and enable them to establish a social order within their family groups. Your rat will also display these behaviors to you when he becomes a member of your family.

# Practical Jokers

Believe it or not, some rats appear to have a sense of humor, and it is common for rats to tease both each other and their humans. My semi-hairless rat Cleo used to sneak up next to me on the couch and pinch the soft part on the back of my arm. I would jump every time, and then she would cock her head and look at me with a twinkle in her eye. Too bad I couldn't hear her laughing!

Priscilla and Richard Taylor of Fremont, California, had a rat named Lassiter who loved to play practical jokes on them to get extra attention. Lassiter was an agouti bareback rat, which means his head was brown and his body was white. He would push all of his bedding to one end of his cage and lay with his head on the bedding and his all-white body on the white plastic bottom of the cage so that it was camouflaged. Priscilla and Richard used to panic because they couldn't see him and thought he had gotten out of the cage and was lost. How clever was that?!

Lassiter also liked to play dead. At one time Priscilla and Richard had another pet rat named Albrecht, who shared the cage with Lassiter. When Albrecht was found motionless on the cage floor, they panicked and rushed to take him out, but it was too late, he was already gone. They think Lassiter remembered how intensely they reacted when they found Albrecht lying there. After that, Lassiter would sometimes lay in exactly the same position in which they found Albrecht, complete with half-closed eyes and his tongue sticking out! The first time he did this, they both screamed and quickly ran to the cage to see if he was really gone. As soon as they opened the cage door, Lassiter jumped up very excited and pleased with himself.

# Chapter 2

# How Smart Are Rats?

fter observing rats for more than 20 years, I think that the average rat is as smart as the average dog. However, I don't think that the smartest rats are as smart as the smartest dogs. You'll find a simple questionnaire in the Appendix that will help you judge the intelligence of your rats.

## RAT INTELLIGENCE

We can gain more insight into the abilities and intelligence of rats by looking at some of the psychological research that has been done on how they learn. While we may not like the idea of rats being used in laboratory experiments, we may as well take a look at what has been published. I'm sure that the rats involved in such research would want other rats to benefit from it. Some of the experiments are quite interesting and even amazing.

For instance, one study that appeared in the news in January 2005 showed that rats can tell the difference between spoken Dutch and Japanese, which means that they have the ability to listen carefully to human speech. I believe that they can even learn the meanings of words.

Several studies suggest that rats can count and even add! In the 1980s, rats were trained to press one lever when they heard two beeps or saw two flashes of light and another lever for either four beeps or four flashes of light. The rats learned this task fairly easily. Then they were tested by being presented two beeps and two flashes of light at the same time. The rats did not press the lever for "two" but instead pressed the lever for "four," indicating that they had added the beeps and flashes together.

### Thoughts and Dreams

As amazing as these experiments are, other tests show that rats can have more complex thoughts and that they even dream. In 1999, physiologist John Chapin, PhD, discovered that rats could learn to control a robotic arm with their thoughts. First, he taught his lab rats to press a lever to get a drink of water. Next, he implanted tiny electrode wires into the part of their brain that controls movement and connected them to a robotic arm. When the rats thought about getting a drink of water, it triggered the robotic arm to bring water to them. There was a look of surprise on the rats' faces at first, but they quickly learned to stop pressing the lever and use their thoughts alone to get a drink of water.

**Studies reveal that rats can have complex thoughts and even dream. Brain scans have shown that they relive the experience of running a maze while asleep.**

In 2001, biologists at the Massachusetts Institute of Technology (MIT) implanted electrode wires into the part of the brain involved in memory. They then trained the rats to run a maze while recording the electronic impulses produced by their brains. Recordings of the brain impulses showed a very specific pattern in each rat every time he ran the maze. The researchers then recorded the brain impulses while each rat was asleep and dreaming. Half of all the dream recordings were an exact match to the patterns seen while each rat ran the maze. The obvious conclusion is that the rats were dreaming about running the maze.

### Robot Rats

In 2002, Dr. John Chapin conducted further studies. He announced that his research team had used electrodes implanted in the rats' brains to control their behavior. One electrode was located in the area of the brain that records satisfaction when needs such as food or water are met. The other wires were placed in the areas of the brain that receive impulses from the rat's whiskers—

one for the right side and one for the left. Chapin found that stimulating the rat's satisfaction center caused him to move forward, whereas stimulating one of the whisker bundles caused the rat to turn to that particular side. Thus, by sending stimulation to the rat's brain, they could guide the rat in any direction. They took this study a step further. They attached a little backpack to each rat containing a battery and a microprocessor that received signals from a laptop computer. The research team felt that someday rats could be trained to wear tiny cameras and directed through stimulation to search for trapped disaster survivors.

After hearing of these experiments, the news media was filled with headlines about "Robot Rats," which resulted in the outrage of many rat lovers. Despite what they believed, however, this experiment did not turn the rats into "robots." Each rat had to undergo up to ten days of training before the signaling could reliably influence his behavior. The stimulation was simply a new way to give commands and rewards. The biggest difference between this method of training rats and the traditional way was that the signals could be given from a distance. It was remote training, not true remote control.

Once a rat was trained, the stimulation could get him to go almost anywhere. These rats were willing to climb a ladder or tree, walk along an

## Movie Star Rats

Rats often appear briefly in television shows and movies to add a scary or creepy atmosphere. However, sometimes rats play a more substantial role in the story. The first movies that used a large number of rats as characters were *Willard* in 1971 and its sequel *Ben* in 1972. I was privileged to meet the man who trained all these rats, Moe DiSesso, known as "The Rat Man."

For *Willard*, Moe trained 600 rats, but special effects made them look like 6,000. He trained different groups of rats to perform different tasks. Some walked up a plank, some were taught to chew through a door by licking peanut butter off of balsa wood, and some were trained to lick peanut butter off of a person to appear as if they were eating a dead body. Moe trained 12 rats to act the part of the lead character Socrates and 13 rats to play the part of Ben. The behavior for which each rat was trained was matched to the rat's personality. Moe went on to train rats for 17 other movies.

I also met the trainers at Animal Actors of Hollywood in Thousand Oaks, California. They trained more than 250 rats for Francis Ford Coppola's 1992 movie *Bram Stoker's Dracula*. Trainer Veronica "Ronni" Wise said that rats are one of the animals she finds most rewarding to train. She loves telling people about rats and how wonderful, intelligent, and talented they are!

Other movies that feature large numbers of live rat "actors" include *Indiana Jones and the Last Crusade* (1989), *The Rats* (a.k.a. *Killer Rats*, 2003), and the 2003 remake of *Willard*. Movies notable for pet rat characters include *The Abyss* (1989), *Home Alone 3* (1997), and *Rat* (2001).

**Rats can be professionally trained to perform a wide variety of tasks. Some of these tasks are entertainment related, but others are educational or have huge benefits for human beings.**

elevated walkway, or jump from varying heights. However, being smart, they refused to jump from a height great enough to be dangerous. While the training and stimulation caused the rats to overcome much of their natural fear, it did not cause them to give up their instinct for self-preservation.

## PROFESSIONAL TRAINING

Rats are now professionally trained to perform a wide variety of behaviors. Some of these are strictly for entertainment, but some of the performances can educate as well. For instance, rats act in television shows, commercials, and cinema, as well as in live shows at theaters, schools, kids' parties, zoos, and museums. They have been trained to do simple tricks such as running along the top of a gate and more complicated ones such as stealing a watch, playing basketball, and even placing different recyclables in the proper containers—a good reminder to humans to take care of the environment!

But some rats are trained to do important jobs that have huge benefits for human beings. They have been trained to pull string through electrical conduits at schools so that  computer wires can be pulled through. They also participate

# University Lab Rats

When university students are studying behavior or learning, and the instructor wants them to have hands-on experience training an animal, rats are usually the subjects of choice. It used to be that nearly every psychology department maintained a breeding colony of rats to supply subjects for such training. The good news is this practice was so interesting that many students felt encouraged to take their rats home as pets after the class was over. However, the vast majority of rats used—hundreds of thousands of them—were euthanized at the end of each semester.

Many years ago, I worked at such a university, caring for the rats in the psychology department lab. I tried to convince the professors to stop using live animals and to switch to a computer-generated program that mimicked the behavior of rats as other universities were doing. Sadly, this change did not occur until several years after I left the job.

Currently, there are still a few schools that use rats, but they now do so in much more humane ways. One of the most interesting programs is offered at Nebraska Wesleyan University in Lincoln, Nebraska. There, psychology students train rats to compete in an event called "Xtreme Rat Challenge." (This event was formerly called "The Rat Olympics" until the International Olympic Committee [IOC] complained.) The individual events for which the rats can be trained include the 5-yard (4.6-meter) dash, 5-yard (4.6-meter) hurdles, tightrope walk, long jump, 5-foot (1.5-meter) rope climb, weightlifting, and speed press. Xtreme Rat Challenge became very popular with the public, and it has even been televised on ESPN. More importantly, the students involved do their best to find homes for all the competing rats after the event.

Moorpark College in Moorpark, California, offers a two-year program for people who want to work with exotic animals. In one of the first-year classes on behavior, students are required to teach a rat to perform an obstacle course. The performance of their trained rat counts toward their grade. Most of the students keep their rats as pets after the final test, or they find good homes for them.

If you are looking for a pet rat, you might want to consider adopting a lab rat from one of these university programs.

**Those rats who have the opportunity to play with other rats in an area equipped with a variety of toys actually grow larger, smarter brains.**

in pet-assisted therapy, helping patients heal or keeping up their spirits. Rats have even been trained to alert people to their own medical situations, such as an imminent muscle spasm or epileptic seizure.

Other exciting jobs that rats have been taught are landmine detection and the identification of medical samples from people suffering from tuberculosis. Both these jobs are currently taking place in Africa, performed mostly by giant African pouched rats. (For more information on the rats trained in Africa, go to www.apopo.org.)

As time goes on and more people learn about rats, including their intelligent and friendly nature and their remarkable abilities, we will probably see more of them trained to assist human beings in significant ways.

## HOW SELF-AWARE ARE RATS?

With their relative intelligence made clear by all that rats can be trained to do, one has to wonder how self-aware they may be. The definition of self-awareness is "awareness of your own individuality." Studies on various animals show that some of them—like the great apes, dolphins, and elephants—seem to be incredibly self-aware. For instance, if a chimpanzee is given a mirror, he will come to realize that the image in the mirror is of himself. If a bit of color is secretly placed on the chimp's face and he is given a mirror, he will immediately begin rubbing at the spot of color on his face. Rats aren't as intelligent as apes, but there is one study that suggests that they do have a certain amount of self-awareness.

In 1974, researchers published a study in which rats were first taught that if they pressed a lever when a buzzer sounded, they would get a reward. Then, each rat was put inside a box equipped with four different levers. Each lever was keyed to a particular behavior and would only deliver a reward if the rat was behaving in a particular way when the buzzer sounded. The four behaviors targeted were sitting immobile, face washing, walking, and rearing. The subjects successfully learned to press the correct lever corresponding to their behavior. This suggests that rats have at least a rudimentary awareness of their own behavior.

## MAXIMIZING INTELLIGENCE

Quite a few studies have shown that rats raised in an impoverished environment (an empty cage) are less intelligent than rats raised in an enriched environment that includes toys and other rats with whom to play. Enrichment actually increases the number of brain cells and connections between them. Ironically, in the laboratory, an impoverished environment is normal, and rats in the enriched environment formed the "experimental group." In the wild, every animal is raised in an enriched environment, and an impoverished environment doesn't exist.

Regretfully, however, thousands of pet rats are raised in impoverished environments. Thousands of mother rats have their babies in tiny cages without any toys, and many pet rats live alone in boring, empty cages. It is so sad to think that an impoverished environment may be the normal situation for most pet rats. However, exposure to an enriched environment has benefits at any age, so it is never too late to add interest and excitement to your own rat's life. Training is a great way to offer your pet rat the physical and mental stimulation he needs, and it's a fun way to strengthen the bond you share.

# Chapter 3

# Training Basics

**A**ll training is based on the principle of cause and effect. An individual—whether human or animal—tends to repeat a behavior that has a pleasant outcome. The positive outcome acts as a reward and reinforces the tendency for the behavior to recur. When this principle is applied to training and the trainer rewards the subject for his behavior, the technique is called positive reinforcement.

If a behavior results in an unpleasant outcome, that behavior will tend to decrease. If a trainer provides the unpleasant outcome, it is called punishment. But punishment is a lot trickier than positive reinforcement. In some instances, what you might consider punishment might not be perceived that way by the subject and might actually increase the unwanted behavior.

For instance, if you have a dog who jumps up on you, you might yell at the dog, thinking that yelling is punishment. However, a dog does not see yelling the same way we do. Yelling is very much like barking, and most dogs do not see barking as punishment. In fact, most dogs see yelling as attention, which is positive reinforcement, so yelling at a dog may actually reward the dog's behavior. In this case, the most effective punishment is to totally ignore the dog. Because dogs want your attention, ignoring them is a form of punishment.

There is another problem with punishment, especially physical punishment. Because it is so unpleasant, punishment can provoke a negative emotion in an animal. Punishment can cause an animal to become afraid of the trainer or of the training situation. Some animals can even become aggressive. An animal who is afraid or aggressive is not receptive to learning.

Positive reinforcement is the best technique for training animals and the only method for teaching tricks. When you want to teach an animal to perform tricks, you need the animal's interest and cooperation, so punishment must be avoided at all costs. Any unpleasant experience will destroy the animal's trust in the trainer and discourage him from wanting to participate in the training process. In this case, only positive reinforcement will bring about the desired response in an animal. Punishment should only be used to eliminate unwanted behaviors and then only in mild forms, such as ignoring the animal or providing a "time-out" by putting the animal away in a cage.

The most effective way to train animals to do tricks is with positive reinforcement in the form of treats.

## USING POSITIVE REINFORCEMENT

The most common positive reinforcement used when training animals is food. Most animals are interested in food, especially food they consider extra tasty. However, there are other rewards or reinforcers that can also be used.

For social creatures—including rats, dogs, and humans—social contact can be highly reinforcing. The opportunity to see or interact with another individual may be extremely positive for them. For instance, scientists have found that rats will work to gain the opportunity to see or visit with another rat. Most animals find the sense of touch pleasurable, so the act of petting an animal can be highly reinforcing.

Because social animals seek the approval of their family members, animals who have bonded to a person will have a desire to please that family member. This is why praise can also be an effective reinforcer.

For intelligent animals who have a sense of curiosity, the opportunity to explore can be highly reinforcing. The chance to interact with a new toy or explore a novel situation is often highly motivating. When given the opportunity, some rats will choose to explore a new environment even over eating. Some will enjoy learning new behaviors simply because they are interesting and fun. These rats can learn new tricks even if they aren't interested in eating the treats you offer.

The advantage to using food as a reward when training animals is that it tends to be a more consistent motivator than other types of rewards. Food is also fairly quick and easy to give to the animal being trained.

It's important that the training subject get his reward immediately after the behavior you want to reinforce. Because of the principle of cause and effect, animals associate events that occur close together in time. You have only one second to get the reward to your rat. If you wait too long before giving the reward, you risk that the rat will perform some other behavior in the meantime, which he will then associate with the reward instead of the behavior you wanted to reinforce.

## SECONDARY REINFORCERS AND CLICKER TRAINING

It can sometimes be difficult to get a food reward to your rat quickly enough after he performs a behavior. In some cases, it will be helpful to teach the rat a secondary or conditioned reinforcer that can be used to signal that a treat is coming. In animal training jargon, a secondary reinforcer is also called a bridge because it bridges the gap between the behavior and the reward.

Because a piece of tasty food is a naturally positive experience for an animal, the food is called a primary reinforcer. To create a secondary reinforcer, you must teach your rat to associate the food with the secondary reinforcer by pairing them. With enough repetition, the secondary reinforcer can in many

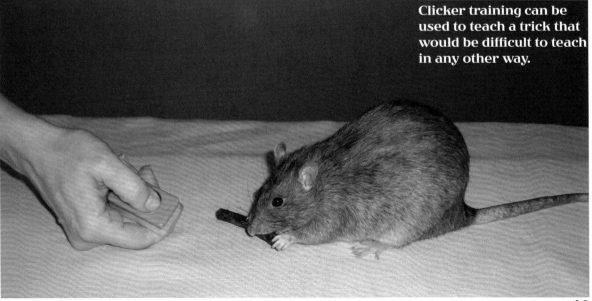

**Clicker training can be used to teach a trick that would be difficult to teach in any other way.**

# Treat Choices of the Stars

When training rats for a movie, veteran rat trainer Moe DiSesso rewarded his animal actors with their normal food by offering them a small dish of grain mix and allowing them to pick out what they wanted. This was the only food his rats were given while being trained, but often work would proceed throughout the day. If the rats weren't going to be trained on a particular day, Moe would still put them in their work situation to eat instead of feeding them in their cage to make sure that they associated work with being fed.

The trainers at Animal Actors of Hollywood reward their rats with granola, sunflower seeds, and monkey chow soaked in water and mashed with a dietary supplement. They also feed them only during training sessions, but they weigh each rat twice a day to make sure that they are getting enough food and are maintaining their normal body weight.

cases become reinforcing on its own. That is, the animal will feel rewarded when he receives the secondary reinforcement and will be satisfied without also receiving the primary reinforcement.

A secondary reinforcer is usually an auditory signal, but it can also be a visual signal or even a physical signal, such as a touch. For instance, at SeaWorld, the bridge used for whales and dolphins is usually a whistle, while the bridge for sea lions is usually a light touch or the word "okay" or "good."

A common secondary reinforcer used by animal trainers, especially dog trainers, is the sound of a clicker. Clickers are popular because they produce a distinctive crisp sound that is the same each time. At first the clicking sound has no meaning for an animal. But when a trainer pairs the sound with food, the animal will start to associate them and learn that the sound means that he will soon be getting a treat.

To teach an animal to associate the clicker with food, you first make the clicking sound and then immediately give the animal a treat. By repeating this action several times, the animal will learn that the clicking sound signals a treat. Again, with enough repetitions, the clicker itself will begin to act as a reinforcer for the animal. It will become a secondary reinforcer.

## REINFORCEMENT SCHEDULES

When first beginning to train a rat to do a trick, food rewards must be used lavishly. The food will help keep the rat's attention and teach him that the training process is pleasurable. To start, treats are given even if the rat does just part of a trick or comes close to doing part of a trick. As the training progresses, treats are used to reward the rat at every step along the way.

Once a trick has been learned, however, another training technique can be used to strengthen the trick behavior. Withholding the reward sometimes, even when the rat does the trick successfully, will actually make him perform the trick more reliably.

This technique is based on a principle scientists discovered when working with rats in the laboratory. They found that when they gave a rat a reward every time he performed a behavior, the rat came to expect the reward. This is called a one-to-one (1:1) schedule of reinforcement. The rat always got one reward each time he did the behavior. If the scientists stopped giving the reward, the rat quickly figured out that the reward was no longer available and stopped doing the trained behavior.

The scientists then started experimenting with different reinforcement schedules. For instance, they began giving a reward for every other time the rat performed the behavior (a 1:2 schedule), every third time (a 1:3 schedule), every fourth time (a 1:4 schedule), etc. They also tried a variable schedule, whereby a computer gave the rat a reward randomly.

A physical cue, such as scratching the top of a jumping platform, will make it easier to teach your rat to jump.

They found that when a rat was put on one of these schedules for a while and then the rewards were stopped, he continued to perform the behavior for a time before giving up. Because the rat had learned he had to perform the behavior more than once to get his reward, he was willing to continue to perform the behavior in the hope that he would eventually get the reward.

The reinforcement schedule that resulted in the most persistent behavior was the variable schedule. When the rats were on this schedule, they did not know how many times they had to perform the behavior before getting their reward. Therefore, when the rewards were discontinued, these rats were willing to perform the behavior for a very long time. In fact, in some cases the rats never gave up!

You can see this principle operating very strongly at gambling casinos. If someone playing a slot machine were to get a payoff every time she pulled the handle and then one time there was no payoff, she would likely switch to another machine or stop playing altogether. But in reality, because the gambler knows that she must play the game an unknown number of times before getting a payoff, she is willing to play quite a long time without any payoff at all.

# Will Work for Their Humans

Students in the exotic animal program at Moorpark College are required to teach a rat to do an obstacle course as part of their final grade. Stacey, one such student, told me that about half of the rats in her lab class became very bonded to their person and were excited about performing the obstacle course. However, some of the rats weren't enthusiastic about the course and only completed it to please their person. Only a few rats were reluctant to perform at all.

Once in training, she also noted that some of the lab rats seemed willing to do the obstacle course for praise and petting only, while others needed food rewards. Stacey wanted her rat to learn without the use of food rewards, but she was only partially successful in training him. Her rat learned to pull down a rope to get a treat in a bucket, ring a bell, and climb several obstacles. However, he failed to learn to push a ball. He also hated doing the tightrope and would stretch his body as far as he could across the rope trying to avoid walking on it, but he did eventually walk the tightrope in the final test. In fact, because it was so clear that her rat hated the tightrope but did it for her anyway, Stacey gained extra points.

When training a rat to do tricks, you can take advantage of this principle by only giving him a treat every other time he performs a trick. You can still reward your rat with praise and verbal encouragement each time. However, you need to apply this principle carefully and only use it once you're sure that your rat has learned the trick well. If skipping treats seems to make your rat less enthusiastic about doing the trick instead of more enthusiastic, you may need to go back to the 1:1 schedule for a while.

## CUES

A cue is a signal you give an animal to tell him what behavior you want him to do. A cue can be an auditory signal, such as a verbal command or a distinct sound, a visual signal, such as a hand movement, or a physical signal, such as a touch on the back. Usually the cue will be selected based on the way the behavior is taught.

For instance, when asking a rat to jump from one platform to another, a good cue is to tap, pat, or scratch the platform where you want the rat to jump. This combines a visual and auditory cue, and it is a very direct cue. The cue suggests the behavior to the rat. In contrast, you could teach the rat to respond to a verbal command, but it would take much longer to teach the trick because the command is not directly related to the behavior.

Another example is the trick of turning in a circle. To teach the trick, you begin by leading the rat in a circle with a piece of food. As he learns the trick, the trainer will be able to raise her hand higher and reduce the size of the circle she makes with her hand. Therefore, the cue that makes the most sense for this trick is a circular hand movement.

The process of reducing or abbreviating the initial training movement until it becomes a cue is called cue fading. The movement gradually fades from being a large complete movement to an abbreviated signal.

In some cases, the equipment used for the trick actually becomes a visual cue. For instance, when you place a rat on a jumping platform, the sight of another platform can be a cue for the rat to jump. Or if you place a rat at the beginning of a tightrope, he will likely see the tightrope as a cue to perform the tightrope walk.

Visual cues are very helpful when training a rat to do a string of tricks, such as an obstacle course. As the rat completes each stage, the next obstacle will act as a cue for him to continue and complete each item in turn.

## METHODS OF TEACHING

There are four different methods of teaching tricks to animals: shaping, molding, leading, and targeting. One method will usually be the best for each trick, depending on the animal and the trick itself.

### Shaping

Shaping is the method used during clicker training. This is a step-by-step method of training that gradually shapes the animal's behavior into

**You can teach a simple physical trick, such as jumping, by leading your rat through the behavior with a treat.**

the specific complete behavior you want. It tends to work well for complex behaviors, but the trainer must be observant and have quick reflexes. This is because you must immediately reward the animal with a click as soon as he performs a behavior you want to reinforce.

To start, you click and reward the animal for whatever behavior he currently does that is closest to the behavior you want him to do. Once the animal is performing that behavior consistently, you stop clicking for that behavior and wait for the animal to try something new. The animal has come to expect the click and reward for that behavior, so when you stop clicking, the animal typically becomes confused and either extends the behavior he has been doing or tries something new.

For example, let's say you want to train a rat to retrieve. You place a new object in front of the rat, such as a small twig, hoping he will approach the item and sniff it. You click and reward the rat for any movement toward the object. When he is consistently approaching the object, you stop clicking and wait for a new behavior.

The rat will usually approach the object, and when you don't click, he will look at you and then look back at the object. If you continue to wait a few seconds, the rat is likely to sniff or touch the object, and then you click and reward. Once the rat is doing this behavior consistently, you wait again, hoping that he will pick up the object in his teeth. This whole process will usually take about five to ten minutes.

The disadvantage of shaping is that you are dependent on the animal's behavior. You can only reward behaviors the animal does spontaneously. If you want to take a more active approach to the training process, you must use one of the other methods.

## Molding

Molding is a training method whereby you physically mold the animal into the behavior you want. For instance, to teach a dog to sit, you physically push down on his rump until he sits. You then reward the dog. Or to teach a dog to shake hands, you lift his foot with your hand. Molding is a very straightforward and simple training method.

There are two disadvantages to the molding method. First, it is suitable only for simple behaviors. Second, some animals react badly to this type of handling. When they are touched, they may become overly excited, playful, and distracted from learning. Or they may become agitated, resistant, fearful, or even aggressive. The molding technique has only a limited application when training rats.

# The Business of A to Bs

The trainers at Animal Actors of Hollywood claim that most of the jobs they get for rats consist of what professionals in the business call "A to Bs." In layman's terms, this means that the rats are trained to run from point A to point B. This behavior is trained using a buzzer. The rats start from a carrying cage and are trained to run to wherever the buzzer is located. It takes an average of six to nine days to train a rat to perform this behavior reliably, but the trainers must then take the rats to the actual film location and practice with them there to make sure that they won't be bothered by the sights, sounds, and smells of the movie set. They will often work with the rats for two weeks on location.

More complicated behaviors, such as jumping to an actor's shoulder or fetching a watch, are called trained behaviors, and these take more time to teach. These behaviors are trained using the clicker method. Trainers will work with 10 to 12 rats and then pick the best 2 or 3 for the actual job. Among a group of rats, you will often find some who make better runners and some who can "hit a mark." Hitting a mark means that the rat learns to go to a particular spot and stay there. For instance, the rat may be trained to go to a small square of wood and sit on it. Later, the trainers may use a piece of tape on the floor as the "mark." It's all very professional!

## Leading

Leading is a method that is halfway between shaping and molding. In this method, you use a piece of food held in your fingers to lead the animal into the behavior you want. A perfect example is the trick we talked about earlier, teaching a rat to turn in a circle. By using the food to lead the rat in a circle, you guide him into the exact behavior you want but without physically touching him. Leading is a technique that works quite well for teaching many tricks to rats.

## Targeting

The final training method, targeting, uses a combination of shaping and leading, but in this case, you don't use food to lead the animal—you use an object called a target. Targeting is used extensively in training marine mammals; the target is usually a ball on the end of a long pole. To start, the target is gently touched to the animal's nose (rostrum). Next, the animal is rewarded with a secondary reinforcer, or bridge, and given a primary reward. Once the animal understands that he will be rewarded when the target touches his nose, the target is positioned a few inches (several cm) from his nose. In most cases, the animal moves to touch the target with his nose. The trainer then moves the target farther and farther away until the animal will approach and touch the target from any distance.

Once the animal understands the principle behind the target, it can then

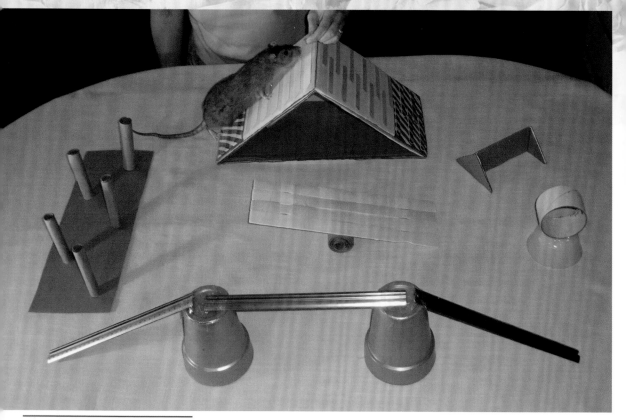

**Chaining is a process of teaching an animal to perform a series of behaviors one after another, such as running an obstacle course.**

be used to guide his movements. This is how a dolphin is taught to leap out of the water. The target is positioned a few feet (about a meter) above the water, and the dolphin is rewarded for touching it. The target is then gradually raised higher and higher until the dolphin is leaping out of the water to touch the target far above the surface of the pool.

A similar type of training, usually called buzzer training, is used for animal actors. In this case, instead of the target being an object that the animal must touch with his nose, it is a buzzer or some other device that makes a sound. The animal is trained to run to the source of the sound from any distance. Often the buzzer is placed inside a box so that the animal runs inside the box. Buzzer training is taught in the same way as target training. Target and buzzer training are most useful for teaching a behavior when you want the animal to move from one place to another. Targeting is a good method to use to teach a rat to run an obstacle course or compete in agility training.

## Chaining

Chaining is a training technique used to teach a series of behaviors you want to occur in order. The most obvious example of this is an obstacle course. Most people think that you want to teach the tricks in the order you want the animal to perform them, but actually you want to teach them in reverse order. You teach the last behavior in the chain first. Once the rat knows that behavior, you teach the behavior that comes just before the last one in the chain, and then you have the rat do the last behavior, which he already knows.

For example, if an obstacle course consists of a tunnel, a ramp, a tightrope, and a jump, you teach the jump first, then the tightrope, then the ramp, then the tunnel. And each time you teach the rat an obstacle, you have him do all the other obstacles that he has already learned in turn.

A very simple example of chaining is the method used at the Sacramento Zoo to teach their performing rats a rope-walking act. In the show I saw, a nautical rope about 2 inches (5.1 cm) thick and about 30 feet (9.1 cm) long ran along the back wall of the stage on which they performed. At each end

**You need to expose your rats to different locations, people, and props to have them perform reliably. Here a rat balances a thimble on his head.**

# Rattie Goes to School

In 1997, Judy Reavis, Vice President of Hermes Systems Management in Benicia, California, was discussing with a colleague the problem of running new wires though the walls and ceilings of schools to connect classroom computers to the Internet. The colleague said that he knew someone who had tried to train a rat to perform this job but was unsuccessful. Reavis thought that perhaps the person who was unsuccessful didn't have the patience to train the animal properly and decided to try it for herself. She adopted an albino female named Rattie from a biophysics experiment in college and decided to try to train her.

Reavis chose targeting to train Rattie, which initially involved teaching her to go to a tapping sound. For example, Reavis would tap on the outside of various obstacles to guide Rattie during training sessions. Later, when Rattie was actually working at job sites, she would follow the tapping sound being made on walls or ceilings. To string wires in schools, Rattie wore a harness with a string attached so that it would be pulled along as she moved forward. Once Rattie found the exit, her job was done and the string was used to pull computer cables into place.

Reavis spent 20 minutes a day training Rattie, whenever her traveling schedule would allow. Because the training wasn't continuous, it took about three months to train her. As a result, Reavis felt that Rattie was pretty easy to train, and it helped that she loved to climb and had a fearless personality.

of the rope was a hole in the stage wall to the backstage area. They started the training by placing the rat a short distance from the end of the rope, encouraging him with food and praise to walk to the end and through the hole, where he got a treat. At each step of the training, they put the rat a little farther from the end so that he had to walk farther on the rope. Finally, they taught the rat to go from the backstage area through the first hole, run the whole length of the rope, and then go through the second hole into the backstage area at the opposite end.

## GENERALIZATION AND DISCRIMINATION

Generalization is the tendency for organisms to react to different stimuli in the same way or in a similar way. This is why a rat who is used to getting treats poked through the bars of his cage may bite a finger that is also poked into the cage.

In training jargon, the opposite of generalization is discrimination. You learn to discriminate when you learn to vary your behavior according to what is happening around you. A rat learning a trick discovers that he gets a treat when he does one behavior, so he begins to repeat that behavior. When the trainer wants to teach another trick, the rat may try to repeat the first trained behavior, only to find that it doesn't result in a reward this time.

Generalization and discrimination can occur in relation to all kinds of stimuli, including location. The stimuli that the rat is responding to may not be limited just to the cues of the trainer but may also include the furniture in the room and the room itself. A rat may learn to perform a trick in one location but fail to generalize this behavior to a new location.

For this reason, if you expect your rats to perform their tricks anywhere else than where you teach the tricks, you need to hold training sessions in different locations. Different locations will present different stimuli that can interfere with the rat's responses in many ways. A new location can be frightening, and a frightened rat will not want to perform. Or the new location can offer new sights and sounds that distract the rat from his training or performance.

The presence of novel elements in a familiar location can also interfere with learning or performing. For instance, some of my rats have been eager to perform their tricks in my living room when we are alone. But when several strangers fill the room, especially with bright lights and a video camera, these rats refuse to perform.

So if you expect your rats to perform for an audience, have them practice those tricks in a variety of different performance situations once they have learned the tricks well. You will need to expose them to different locations, people, sounds, lights, and smells for them to perform reliably.

## OBSERVATIONAL LEARNING

Rats can learn by observing the behavior of other rats. For instance, if one rat sees another rat take the top off of a container and get a treat, he may try to do it too. In the same way, rats can learn a trick by watching another rat perform it.

**Rats can partially learn a trick by watching another rat perform it, but they will need to practice it themselves to become proficient.**

For observational learning to take place, you must follow four steps. First, the student must pay attention to the model and be actively watching. Second, the student must be able to remember what he saw. Third, the student must be motivated to imitate the action he observed. Finally, the student must practice the action himself. Just watching is not enough to teach the muscles and nerves how to perform a task.

So a rat who watches a trick may not be able to immediately perform the trick himself, but he may be able learn that trick more easily than if he had never seen it performed. So if you plan to teach tricks to more than one of your rats, it is a good idea to conduct your training in a location that is in view of the other rats.

Observational learning can also help a rat refine his technique when performing a trick. After I taught my semi-hairless Dumbo rat Gideon to do the basket pull-up trick (see Chapter 7), I decided to teach the trick to his roommate, Two Tone. Two Tone wasn't the brightest rat I've ever had, but in five lessons he was pulling up the string to get the treat in the basket. (Gideon learned it in three lessons.)

Initially, Two Tone didn't have very good technique—he leaned too far over the edge of the stool and therefore had trouble pulling the basket all the way up onto it. I decided to let him watch Gideon perform the trick because he had great technique. Gideon would stand back from the edge and pull the basket up onto the stool smoothly and quickly.

I then put the two rats on the stool together, and of course Gideon immediately pulled up the basket. Although it didn't appear that Two Tone was paying much attention, I let Gideon do the trick two more times, and then I moved him over to the couch and asked Two Tone to do the trick. This time he pulled up the string the way Gideon did it! Obviously, he had learned the new technique from watching Gideon. What a great demonstration of the rat's intelligence (even one who wasn't particularly bright)!

# Chapter 4

# Practical Training

**A**lthough trick training can be enjoyable for both you and your rat, practical training that can keep your pet safe and secure is much more important. Proper training and handling can strengthen the bond between you and your pet, which is an important precursor to any type of training. However, the first thing a pet should learn from his owner is that he can trust her to be patient, consistent, and caring. Later, after the basics have been established, you can teach your rat some tricks and share many fun activities together.

## TRUST TRAINING

A rat who is extremely shy or even afraid of humans may be that way due to several factors. In most cases, it is simply that the rat didn't receive enough socialization as a baby. But in rare cases, it's possible that the rat may have been abused. A rat can also genetically inherit a tendency to be shy or nervous, and such an individual will obviously be more affected by a lack of socialization. For example, rats with the agouti color gene tend to be more anxious than those with the nonagouti color gene, but this can be overcome with proper socialization.

Regardless of the cause of a rat's fear or shyness, trust training can be highly effective in helping him to become accustomed to human contact. I learned a very simple taming technique from a member of my national rat club, Elizabeth R. TeSelle, and I've used it with all my distrustful new rats ever since. Years ago, she adopted a rat named Phineas who was terrified of humans. The only way Phineas had been previously handled by his former owners was by being hoisted in the air by the tail. Ouch! The first time Elizabeth reached her hand into his cage with a treat, he shrieked in terror and ran into the corner, where he huddled and chattered in fear. Phineas ended up biting both her and her husband Marc several times before they finally saw the need to develop their trust training technique. But once he learned that his new family wasn't going to hurt him and was much more understanding of his needs, he became a totally trusting companion, climbing into their laps for attention, riding on their shoulders, and grooming Marc's beard.

The most dramatic case for which I used trust training was with a rescue rat who was so frightened of people he would dash for his nest box to hide whenever he saw anyone. But using the trust training approach, it took only three days before this poor guy would willingly come out of his cage to be held and petted.

The first thing a pet should learn from his owner is that he can trust her to be patient, consistent, and caring.

## Preparation

The most important key to the trust training technique is to use soft food on a spoon as both a lure and reward. Using the soft food prevents your rat from being able to grab it and run away with it. He is forced to stay near you to lick it off the spoon. Also, you will be at an advantage when dealing with an extremely fearful rat because he may feel the need to defend himself by biting, in which case he will bite the spoon and not your finger.

Foods you can use include yogurt, baby foods, mashed banana, mashed avocado, etc. Rats have a tendency to be suspicious of new foods, and many unsocialized rats have not been exposed to a variety of different things to eat. If the rat shows no interest in the food you are using, put a bit of it in a dish in the cage (jar lids make great rat dishes) to allow him to try it at his leisure. Once he is eating the food out of the dish, you can use it on the spoon. If your rat still is not interested in eating the food off the spoon, keep trying different foods until you find one he likes. In severe cases in which a rat refuses to eat the special food from the spoon, you may have to reduce the amount of his regular food so that he will be hungrier than usual.

## Trust Training Basics

The best time to have a training session is when your rat is alert and a bit hungry.

- To begin, offer your rat the special food treat on the spoon inside his cage.
- When he will comfortably eat it inside the cage, have him come to the door of the cage to get it.
- Next, have him get up onto the door (depending on the design of the cage) to get the food.
- Once he does this reliably, have him come out of the cage and climb on your knee, arm, or other hand before allowing him to eat the food.
- Next, require that he let you pick him up and put him on your knee, arm, or hand before giving him his treat.

When a rat allows you to pick him up, hold him, and pet him while remaining relaxed, he has developed a real sense of trust and will respond to handling like a rat who has been well socialized. At this point, you can discontinue the trust training.

# What's in a Name?

When choosing a name for a pet rat, many people like to choose a simple one- or two-syllable name that is quick and easy to say. Short names do seem to be easier for animals to learn. Other people like more creative choices. How about Obi-Wan Skinobi for a hairless rat? Of course, you'd probably end up calling him Obi for short!

Some of my favorite names for ratties are Moses, Lily, Milo, Bella, Dixie, Joey, Vinnie, Gonzo, Zorro, Tico, Cricket, and Bubba. I have also given two of my rats the name "rat" in a foreign language: Mooshé from Farsi (Persian) and Gimoo from the Polynesian language of Nukuoro. In many European languages, the word "rat" is similar to English. It is ratte in German; rotte in Norwegian and Danish; rott in Estonian; rata in Swedish, Italian, and Spanish; rat in French; and ratazana in Portuguese. Here is how to say "rat" in some other languages:

| | | | |
|---|---|---|---|
| Arabic—fahr fara | Hausa (Nigeria)—bira or | Lao—nu | Russian—krisa |
| Basque—arratoi | kusu | Maori (New Zealand)— | Swahili—panya |
| Cayapa (Ecuador) —iyu | Hawaiian—iole | kiore | Thai—nŏo |
| Chinese—lao see | Hungarian—patkany | Maranoa (Phillipines)—ria | Vietnamese—chuot |
| Choco (Panama)—cado | Indonesian—tikus | Polish—szczur | Welsh—ffrengig |
| Croatian—loviti | Japanese—nezumi | Punjabi (India)—chŭha | |
| Cuna (Panama)—nusa | Kikuyu (Kenya)—mbia | Quechua (Inca)—ucucha | |
| Czech—krysa | Korean—jwee | Romanian—Shobolan | |

## THE NEXT IMPORTANT LESSON: COME WHEN CALLED

Every rat should be taught to come when called in case he accidentally gets out of his cage, especially if he hides or heads toward a hazardous place. This behavior is more than a trick; it can be a lifesaver in some circumstances. Most rats will learn their name and come to you when you call them just through normal daily interaction, but it's good to hold some formal training sessions to make sure that your pet learns this lesson well. Only by constant repetition will the response become automatic. When well trained, your rat will be more likely to respond to your call even if fear is telling him to stay hidden.

### Teaching Your Rat to Come When Called

To teach your rat to come when called, prepare the rewards you will use during training. These can be any foods your rat likes. If you are going to repeat the lessons several times, you should use very small pieces of food. (See Chapter 5.) You can also use soft food on a spoon.

- Start the first lesson by saying your rat's name to get his attention focused on you. (Your rat will learn his name faster if you always say it when you greet and pet him.)
- Next, say his name and the word "treat," then immediately give him the food reward. When your rat seems to understand that he will get a reward when you say the word "treat," you can move on to the next step in the training.
- Once your rat reliably responds to the previous exercise, he will be interested in pursuing food rewards associated with other exercises. So now, instead of handing your rat the treat, hold it a few inches (several cm) away so that he has to come to your hand to get it. Say his name and "Come get treat."
- Gradually make him travel longer distances to get the treat until he will run across the couch, table, bed, or floor to receive it.

It's a good idea to practice this behavior often at first so that your rat learns it well, and then continue to practice it occasionally to keep it fresh in his mind.

Another behavior I have found very helpful to teach my rats is to have them climb in and out of an open basket to make it easier for me to carry them places. I usually have between 12 to 24 rats who live in different groups. Whenever I would get a group of rats out for playtime, I used to get scratched up trying to carry several rats at a time from their cage to the couch and back. They didn't mean to scratch me, but sooner or later someone would lose their balance and my hand or arm would be scratched as a result.

I finally got the idea to buy a basket with a handle that was big enough

**Every rat should be taught to come when called. Learning this lesson well may save your rat's life someday.**

to hold about five rats. Now, whenever it's time to take them out of the cage, I just hold the basket up to the open door and say "Get in." If they're slow to get in, I might need to nudge one of them in or sometimes even pick one up and put him in the basket. The rats sit calmly in the basket while I carry them to the couch. Then I say "Out," and they will usually pile out quickly, happy to be unconfined. It really didn't take too much training for most of the rats to get used to this routine. I was actually amazed how fast they learned it. It seemed as though some of them understood my purpose right from the beginning, although others did need a bit more encouragement and training. Now getting all my rats out for playtime is pain-free.

## AVOIDANCE TRAINING

Now that you have established a trusting relationship with your rat (or rats), you have probably already discovered how much fun it is to have him out of the cage, either to play with him or just to let him spend some time with you. However, the biggest problem with giving rats freedom in the house is their tendency to chew on things. Some rats are very well behaved and never chew on furnishings, while other will gnaw on everything.

The most effective way to prevent chewing is to remove any items you don't want chewed. In some cases, a rat may not chew in most areas but may be attracted to a certain object he loves to gnaw every chance he gets. If you can't remove the item from the rat's reach, perhaps you can physically block it off by putting up a barrier. For instance, you can cut open a large cardboard box, fold it flat, and stand it up with the top and bottom flaps facing the rat. With the bottom flaps weighted down with bricks or heavy cans, a rat will find it difficult to get around such a barrier. If neither of these solutions is an option, there are two types of avoidance training I can recommend trying: aversion training and time-out training.

### Aversion Training

One of my rats, Lily, learned how to go behind the couch cushion, where she would happily sit and chew into it to make a little hidey hole for herself. Every time I found her there, I immediately removed her and placed her back in her cage, but this did nothing to change her pesky behavior.

I finally resorted to buying a spray product designed to repel pets from any area that is sprayed with it. I applied it to the area behind the couch cushion

# Rat-Proofing Your House

If you want to give your rats freedom to roam your house, carefully rat-proof each room to which you give them access.

- Inspect the cupboards and cabinets, and if you find any access holes in the kick spaces, seal them.
- If you allow your rats in the kitchen, you must block off access around the refrigerator, stove, and dishwasher. Rats entering these areas might be tempted to chew on water lines or electrical cords.
- Make sure that heater vent covers are secure.
- Secure electrical cords up out of reach.
- In the bathroom, keep the lid of the toilet closed.
- Store all medications, cleaners, and other products out of reach. Keep your rats out of areas where pesticides have been applied.
- Move valuables out of rooms to which your rat will have access.
- Rats like to burrow in piles of clothing, so inspect them before putting them in the laundry or into closets. Rats can also get caught inside upholstered furniture when humans sit down or get up. Recliners are particularly dangerous.
- Keep cigarettes, ashtrays, and candy out of reach. It's best not to smoke around rats because it will aggravate respiratory infections.
- When rats are loose on the floor, wear only socks or slippers—if you accidentally kick or step on one of your rats, a shoe-clad foot can kill him.

and continued to use it every night before I let my rats out on the couch. The spray did not smell unpleasant to me, and at first it did not seem to deter Lily. However, over a period of about two weeks, she spent less and less time behind the cushion, and she eventually stopped going back there at all. So this product does work by making the object something your rat would rather avoid, although it is not an immediate fix.

There are other safe chemical products designed to prevent chewing through avoidance, but they do so by tasting unpleasant rather than by keeping the pet away from an area because it smells unpleasant. Some of these products include sprays and pastes that are applied directly to the object or surface being chewed. I found that a few of my rats actually seemed to like the taste of the bitter paste!

But there is a drawback even to products that the rats don't like: Rats can gnaw on objects without tasting them. A rat's mouth is designed with special cheek folds that keep gnawed material from entering the mouth cavity. By the time the rat tastes the product, he has already taken a chunk out of the protected object. Therefore, these products are of limited use to prevent unwanted chewing. It is probably better to use a product with an unpleasant smell, or better yet, try another method of prevention training.

There are other methods of avoidance training that may work with rats. You can buy electronic devices designed to keep animals away from an area by producing a loud noise or administering a very mild static shock, but I have not tried these for rats. I would be afraid that the rat would chew on the device and be harmed!

For rats who chew on everything, no amount of training can prevent them from damaging furnishings. If you still want to give rats such as these the freedom to roam around a designated room, you need to either accept the damage they do or extensively rat-proof the area. Rats prefer to chew on the edges of objects and rarely chew on flat surfaces unless there is a dent or hole for them to focus on, so the edges of things need the most protection. The edges of doorjambs and furniture can be protected with metal corner moldings. Baseboards can be protected by just removing them. You can also place a strip of material at least 1 foot tall (30.5 cm), such as metal flashing, around the perimeter of the room.

If a rat wants to get out of a room badly enough, he will concentrate on chewing the door and doorjambs, as well as any carpeting near the door. These areas can be difficult to protect. It is easier to determine why the rat wants out of the room and eliminate that reason. Rats usually want to get out of a room when their owners leave them to play in a room by themselves, and then the rats try to get out to find them. The solution is to only let your rats play out of their cage when you can be in the room with them.

**Time-out training can be used to correct unwanted behaviors. A time-out cage should be small and empty, giving the rat nothing with which he can entertain himself.**

### Time-Out Training

If a rat is focused on chewing just one item or area, you can try using time-out training to correct the unwanted behavior. This method may take a while to work, depending on the rat's personality, so be patient and persistent.

This technique is actually quite simple, so you can easily apply it to a variety of concerns.

Here it is in a nutshell: Every time your rat enters a forbidden area, you must immediately put him in a "jail" cage for a time-out. It doesn't work very well to put him back in his home cage for the time-out because it would offer him too many pleasant diversions. You want the time-out cage to be as boring as possible—just a small empty cage with a water bottle. Whenever your rat approaches the forbidden area, grab him immediately and put him in the jail cage. Leave him there for at least 15 minutes, and then let him out to play again; or if playtime is over, put him back into his home cage. Of course, to correct your rat's inappropriate behavior using this approach, you must first be present to catch him in the act.

Here is an example of how I used time-out training in my home. In a corner of the living room, I kept a child's wading pool, which was a habitat for my two guinea pigs. At that time I also had three rats, two males and a female, who would jump down off the couch to explore the living room during playtime. Eventually, each of them learned how to jump into the guinea pig habitat and unfortunately began to bother and even bite the guinea pigs.

In what seemed like a vain attempt to prevent the pets from becoming injured, I would immediately grab a rat every time he jumped into the guinea pig habitat and put him into the jail cage, where he had to stay for the rest of his playtime (usually an hour). One of the males, Negis, learned to avoid the pool within a few days, although I still had to give him a verbal warning if I saw him contemplating invading the pool. Lightning learned to avoid the pool after a few weeks of the jail treatment. Peaches, the female, didn't seem to be able to help herself, though. She continued to jump into the guinea pig habitat night after night, forfeiting her playtime every day. I finally gave up, and instead of putting her in the jail cage, I put her back on the floor. She seemed to find bodily removal enough of a deterrent and afterward would stay out of the guinea pig habitat for the rest of the evening.

## SYSTEMATIC DESENSITIZATION

Sometimes an unwanted behavior is produced by a strong emotion, such as fear or aggression. An example of this would be a dog who is frightened of thunder. Systematic desensitization is a long-term training process that aims to eliminate the emotional reaction animals may have to things that frighten them.

With rats, systematic desensitization can be helpful if they are scared by certain situations or intimidated by another animal or rat. Likewise, it can also be helpful when used with rats who chase other animals, such as cats or dogs.

The basic premise behind this method of training is that an animal will not eat when he is experiencing high emotional arousal. Therefore, if you can get the animal to eat when he is stressed, you will reduce the amount of emotion he is experiencing. By working to reduce the animal's emotional level while gradually exposing him to the situation that evokes the fear or aggression, you can eventually train him to remain calm in that stressful situation.

Keep in mind that because this type of training can take a long time, the subject will be given a high number of treats—so choose one that is healthy and low in fat. The ideal treat is tiny pieces of a fruit or vegetable. Pieces of cereal can also work well, as can tiny pieces of bread or fat-free crackers.

### Desensitizing an Aggressive Rat

To see how the desensitization process works, let's use the example of a rat who is aggressive toward another pet, such as a cat.

Before you start, choose an appropriate location in which to conduct the training. This should be a place where the target situation (aggression toward the cat) occurs or is likely to occur often. In this case, because the cat is more likely to be bothered while the rat is out of his cage playing, let's choose the living room floor as our target zone.

During systematic desensitization, it is very important to be in constant control of the entire situation. Make sure that your rat is only exposed to the cat when you can supervise every aspect of their interaction. There must be no chance that the cat can walk into the room of her own accord. All other pets in the house must also be confined while the training is occurring.

During the session, you will need two people: one to work with the rat and one to control the cat. This is because it will be necessary to have someone

# Rats and Other Pets

Wild rats are predatory animals who will instinctively attack and/or kill other animals smaller than themselves. Therefore, as a precaution, pet rats should not be allowed around other tiny pets such as hamsters, mice, lizards, or birds. (Rats have been known to pull mice through the bars of their cage to kill them!) Some even have a tendency to bully larger pets such as rabbits and guinea pigs and so should not be allowed to interact with them unless supervised. In many cases, rats can coexist with cats and dogs, but it is not recommended that they interact without supervision. On the other hand, some cats and dogs cannot be trusted with rats and may harm or kill them. Pet rats who share a household with cats, dogs, or ferrets should be housed in secure cages and allowed out for playtime only under human observation.

bring the cat into the room at the appropriate time and keep her in a specific spot. As long as the rat stays calm, the cat can be brought closer and closer to him. If the rat shows any signs of becoming aggressive, the cat must immediately be moved away until the rat relaxes. At certain points, the cat may need to be removed from the rat's view, especially early in the training.

**Sometimes an unwanted behavior is produced by a strong emotion, such as fear or aggression. Systematic desensitization is a training process in which the subject is rewarded with treats for remaining calm in a stressful situation.**

## Desensitization Basics

Now that you have chosen your training location and treats, have the assistance of a helper, and have both pets ready to go, you can begin the training session:

- To start, sit in the middle of the room holding your rat. You might want to put him on a harness and leash.
- Give your rat a treat.
- Next, have the other person bring the cat into the room, but position her as far away from your rat as possible.
- If your rat stays calm, continue to give him treats, and try moving the cat 1 foot (30.5 cm) closer. At each step, give your rat a treat to keep

him calm and praise him for being good.

- Continue gradually moving your cat closer as long as your rat stays calm. If he shows signs of aggression, move the cat back until your rat calms down again. You may have to remove the cat from the room. Once your rat is calm again, you can give him more treats.
- If your rat shows aggression but calms down when the cat is moved away, you can again try bringing the cat a little closer but not as close as before. (If your rat continues to be very aggressive and cannot calm down, discontinue the session and try again later.)
- As the session progresses and your rat remains calm with a person holding the cat quite close, let the cat walk around on the floor. Start with the cat on the far side of the room, and gradually let her get closer. Continue giving your rat the treats as you did during the first part of the session.

Each training session should only last about 5 to 15 minutes, depending on the reaction of your rat (and the cat!). You should hold at least one session a day and eventually work up to two or three sessions a day. The entire

**Pet rats who share a household with cats, dogs, or ferrets should be housed in secure cages and allowed out for playtime only under supervision.**

**Always introduce rats to each other for the first time in a neutral area where neither animal will feel defensive about protecting his territory. When they can interact peacefully during several play sessions, it's safe to keep them together.**

desensitization process can take from a few days to several weeks. Eventually, your rat should be able to sit calmly while the cat walks by.

## Desensitizing a Fearful Rat

A more common situation that creates behavior issues is caused by a rat who behaves territorially (aggressively) toward another rat in his group. This can occur if the introduction between the two rats was rushed or if a male rat reaching maturity became aggressive toward his roommates due to a testosterone surge. The victim can develop a lasting fear of the aggressor after being attacked several times or even after just one incident if it was hostile. This fear can persist even after the aggressor is no longer acting aggressively toward the victim.

In this case, the subject is the fearful rat and the target is the formerly aggressive rat, but the desensitization process is the same:

- The first step is to choose the location for the therapy. In this case, start in a location where the subject (the fearful rat) feels comfortable, such as in a play area, but not in the subject's cage. Start by giving the subject treats in the play area.
- Have a second person hold the target rat (the formerly aggressive rat) several feet (1 to 2 meters) away. If the subject shows any sign of fear, move the target rat farther away until the subject calms down.
- When the subject is calm, continue giving him treats.

- Move the target rat closer to the subject only a few inches (several cm) at a time. At each step, make sure that the subject is remaining calm and continuing to eat the treats. If he stops eating and looks worried, move the target rat back until the subject relaxes and begins to eat again.
- Once the subject remains calm when the target rat is held only a few inches (several cm) away, let the target rat walk around in the playground. At this stage, you must also watch the target rat closely to make sure that he does not show any signs of aggression. If he does, you must stop the therapy until the target rat no longer shows aggression toward the subject.
- Eventually, the subject should remain calm when the target rat approaches him.

If you want the two rats to live together, you must continue the therapy with the rats together in the cage. Do not leave the two rats together in the cage unsupervised until they can spend at least half an hour together under supervision without either one showing aggression or fear.

## INTRODUCING NEW RATS

If you have lived with only one rat or have raised your rats together, you may never have had to introduce a new rat to the family group. As already discussed, introductions that have not been handled properly can have serious consequences, so it's vital that this process be undertaken with care. Most adult rats will not immediately accept a strange rat. Instead, they will defend their territory and try to chase off or attack the stranger. This means that the introduction of a new rat must be done slowly.

The willingness of a rat to accept a new roommate depends on his personality, age, and gender. It is generally easier to introduce a new rat to young rats who have not yet matured to the point of defending their territory, or to elderly rats who have mellowed with age. It can take more time—sometimes up to several weeks—to introduce a newcomer to adult rats, but it can be done. With time and patience, almost any rat will accept a new rat.

When introducing a new rat to a group of rats, usually only the dominant resident rat will be aggressive toward the newcomer at first. This is the dominant rat's "job." Once the new rat is accepted by the dominant rat, the others may show some aggression in turn, but it usually won't be as severe.

### Choosing the Newcomer

The easiest introduction is between two young rats, while the most difficult is between two adult males, especially if they aren't neutered. A young rat is the best choice of new roommate for an adult male, but the newcomer

# Stopping a Fight

There are three ways to stop a rat fight. You can first try startling the combatants by clapping loudly near them and yelling "Stop it!" It can also be very effective to startle them by blowing on them as hard as you can. If those approaches don't work, you can try to grab the base of the tail of one of the fighters. Do not grab the tip of the tail, as the skin will slip off. The base of the tail is quite strong, however. You must quickly pull the rat away from his opponent and hoist him up in the air to stop the fight. Then quickly place him in another area. Do not place the rat on your body or grab the rat's body because you will likely be bitten.

should be at least six weeks old. This is because adult males will sometimes kill strange baby rats younger than this. (Note: This instinctive behavior is of benefit to a wild rat who is looking for a new territory. If he finds a strange female with babies, killing the babies will encourage the female to come into estrus so that the new male can sire his own offspring. In a colony situation, this killing behavior is suppressed by the act of mating and the pheromones of the pregnant female. Because there are always pregnant females in the colony and the males mate frequently, colony babies are not killed by the males.)

**When adding new rats to the family group, the easiest introduction is between two young rats or a young rat and a adult male.**

During the introduction process, you should only advance to the next step if there is no sign of aggression within the recommended time. If a session results in aggression, try again later or go back a step.

### Aggressive Signals

Because you want to avoid any fighting during the early stages of the introduction process, you must recognize behaviors that may indicate a potential squabble.

Male and female rats both express aggression by puffing up their fur and arching their backs. Rats who are hairless, semi-hairless, or rex will not exhibit the puffed fur, so you have to watch very carefully for the arched back posture.

Sometimes an aggressive rat will quickly attack another rat. In other situations, he will first sidle over to him and push a shoulder against his body as a test of strength and as a signal that he plans to attack. If you see a rat giving signals of aggression, do not pick him up because he might bite you. Instead, immediately remove the rat who is in danger of being attacked. If you must pick up an aggressive rat, wrap him in a thick towel.

When two rats are having a mild disagreement and they aren't quite sure who is dominant, or if a subordinate rat does not want to give in to a more dominant rat, they may stand on their hind legs and box.

If a fight does occur, the rats will grapple and roll around while scratching at each other and trying to bite one another. If the fight isn't really serious, it may only last a few seconds and then the attacker will allow the vanquished

# Litter Box Training

Rats can be very easy to litter box train. Many have a natural tendency to use a litter box because it's instinctive for them to use one place as a toilet. In the wild, rats use one room in their burrow as a toilet. Some rats will use a litter box exclusively, but others seem to go out of their way to avoid using the box. I think that a rat's bathroom habits have a lot to do with the habitat in which he grew up as a baby, as well as the bathroom habits of his mother. A rat who is raised in a small cage with a mother who has poor bathroom habits may never learn to use a litter box. On the other hand, rats raised in a large area equipped with litter boxes, with a mother who uses the boxes, will naturally become litter box trained.

The best way to assure that your rats will use a litter box is to make sure that the box is easy to access. Some rats are lazy and won't make the extra effort to get to an inconvenient box. In a multistory cage, you may need a litter box on each floor. Place it in a spot your rats are most likely to use as a toilet anyway. The most common places are a corner of the cage or right outside their sleeping area.

You can use a variety of litter products in the litter box. It's a good idea to use a different product in the litter box than what you use on the floor of the cage. One of my rat fan club members reported that her female rats were not good about using a litter box until she started using a clumping cat litter in the box. Then they started using the litter box almost exclusively. Clumping cat litters must be used with extreme caution, however, because if a rat tries to eat it, it will react to their saliva by clumping and can get caught in their mouth or throat, causing a serious choking hazard. If you want to use a clumping litter, observe your rats carefully for several hours after putting it in their cage to make sure that they do not try to eat it.

Outside the cage, the litter box should be near an area your rats tend to spend most of their time. If your rat is on the couch with you, you can't expect him to leave the couch to go to a litter box. Have a small litter box right on the couch. More than one litter box might be required in a room, and corners are usually preferred places for elimination.

If your rats learn to use a litter box in their cage first, they might be more likely to use a litter box outside their cage. The secret to training your rats to use a litter box in the cage is to inspect the cage frequently and move any wet litter and feces into the litter box. Eventually, your rats will get the idea that the litter box is the designated latrine.

If you are observant, you will learn to recognize the characteristic posture of a rat getting ready to relieve himself. If you see your rat assume this posture outside the litter box, you can pick him up and gently place him in the box. Try not to scare him or startle him too much. Praise him for using the box.

Bringing a new rat into the household can cause a litter box-trained rat to "forget" his training. In one case, after I introduced a new rat to the group, my neutered male hairless rat Gimoo (his name means "rat" in a Polynesian language), who was the dominant rat, started eliminating next to me on the couch, something he had never done before. This is a type of marking behavior, and Gimoo was probably trying to inform the new rat that the couch and I were his territory. One night I noticed Gimoo assuming the position next to me, so I picked him up and put him in the litter box. He returned to my side and again assumed the position. Once again I placed him in the litter box. The third time he finally relented and used the litter box. Of course, I praised him highly. Gimoo gradually returned to using the litter box as the new rat became integrated into the group. Eventually, he no longer felt that he needed to mark his territory.

When introducing rats, you should have a separate cage for the newcomer to live in at first.

to escape without actual injuries. However, in a more serious fight, the animals may receive fairly severe bite wounds. These often occur in the shoulder area, where the skin is thickest. However, if a male is really intent on injuring an opponent, he will sometimes bite him in the groin as if trying to castrate him. Fortunately, rats have few pain nerve endings in their skin and often do not appear to feel discomfort, even from large skin wounds. Usually, most wounds will heal up quickly on their own.

## The Introduction Process

When introducing rats, you should have a separate cage for the newcomer to live in at first. The introduction process consists of several steps, and the time required for each may vary.

- The first step is to place the cages near each other so that the rats can see and smell each other. Place them far enough apart so that they can't reach through the bars to the other cage, or they may try to bite each other's toes or tail. You can move on to the next step when none of the rats expresses any aggression toward the individual in the adjoining cage.

- Next, switch the rats to each other's cage for 30 to 60 minutes to allow them to explore each other's areas. This gives them firsthand experience with each other's scent. You may have to do this several times. You can move on to the next step when none of the rats expresses aggression when smelling the other individuals' scents in their own cage.

- Following this, introduce the rats to each other in neutral territory, which should be someplace where the resident rats are not used to playing. Your bathtub is a good place. This will give them a chance to become acquainted without the residents feeling the need to defend their territory. Another technique that can work is to take the rats for a short car ride in a neutral carrier. You can move on to the next step when there is no aggression after 15 to 30 minutes.

- Now let them interact in an area where the residents are used to playing. Watch them carefully because this is where some fighting may break out. It may help if you put the new rat(s) in your lap along with the other rats. By holding everyone at the same time, it may tell the residents that you have already accepted the new rat(s). In most cases, you will need to repeat this step several times, ending the session as soon as any of the rats starts showing signs of aggression. You can move on to the next step when all the rats interact peacefully during several sessions in the play area for at least half an hour per session.

- The final step is to clean the larger cage out completely and rearrange the furnishings so that it appears to be a new cage. Trim the back toenails of the rats to minimize scratching in a scuffle. Smear some yogurt on the rats to keep them busy licking each other. Then put them in this new cage. The best time to do this is in the morning, when they tend to be sleepy.

One of the rats may bully a newcomer, forcing him over on his back. If you've followed the introduction process correctly, don't rush to take the new rat out. Instead, carefully watch the fight. Observe whether the resident rat is showing raised hair, an arched back, or the sideways approach, which are signs of aggression. If so, immediately remove the newcomer, but if not, leave them together.

The resident rat must establish his dominance, and it's normal for him to "beat up" the newcomer. Just because the new rat is squeaking doesn't mean that he's getting hurt. This is just a rat's way of saying "I give up." As long as you have followed the introduction process step by step, and as long as the bullying rat isn't showing signs of aggression, you should let the scuffle run its course. If you take the new rat out, you'll prolong this adjustment phase.

However, if it appears that the new rat is being injured, or if the attack seems especially vicious, then of course you should remove him from the cage. In most cases, the struggle will be over quickly. The dominant resident rat may beat up a newcomer frequently for the first few days, and you shouldn't interfere as long as there are no injuries. Although the first attack is usually the worst, the rats will typically become the best of friends before long, sleeping together and grooming each other.

Because rats are individuals with their own personalities, two rats will occasionally take a disliking to each other and constantly pick on each other. In some cases, this means that the pecking order is changing and the quarrelling will stop eventually. Neutering any males involved will usually solve the problem. However, if these squabbles continue for more than a few weeks, such rats should be separated permanently.

# Chapter 5

# Preparing for Trick Training

**A**ccording to most professional rat trainers, individuals of both genders have the potential to be good performers. While most female rats tend to stay more active all their lives and many male rats tend to get lazier as they age, the ability to be a good performer is more dependent on personality than gender or age.

Nevertheless, there are a variety of factors to take into account when choosing which individuals to train. For example, if you want your rats to perform in public, those with outgoing personalities will tend to do best. A shy rat is unlikely to want to perform in front of strangers. For performance situations, rats who are friendly and people-oriented, rather than those who are independent, will want to interact with and please their trainer. It also helps if the rats are food-oriented, willing to do almost anything for a treat!

Aside from personality, whether a rat will perform well also depends on the type of tricks you want him to do. An active rat will tend to perform better doing more athletic tricks, such as jumps, obstacle courses, basketball, etc. However, a lazy rat will perform better doing tricks in which you need him to stay in place, such as riding in a vehicle. Choose the tricks based on the performer's temperament and level of skill.

## PERFORMERS: MADE, NOT BORN?

The personality of a rat will be influenced by the early socialization he receives. Baby rats who are handled a lot and exposed to a lot of different people will tend to be more outgoing than rats who are handled very little. Handling should start as soon after birth as possible—the more the babies are handled, the better.

In addition, to produce rats who will perform well in public, it is very important that they be exposed to as many different environments as possible while they are babies. The more situations they experience as youngsters, the more comfortable they will be in public later. In a way, performers are made, not born, so you'll want to carry your young rats around with you to all kinds of places.

However, personalities are also strongly influenced by genetics, and some rats will be too shy or independent—even with extensive socialization—to want to perform in public. Shy or independent rats,

The ability to be a good performer is more dependent on personality than gender or age. Rats who are confident and have outgoing personalities tend to do best.

especially if they are food oriented, may be willing to do tricks at home with patient training.

Different professional trainers have varying opinions on the best age to begin training rats. Lynda Lawrence, who owns Pet-Shows-on-Wheels and gives shows at kids' parties, begins her training with five-week-old babies, teaching them to climb a rope. Gary Miller, a trainer at Disney's Animal Kingdom who specializes in elephants, trained rats to do a recycling show for the Pacific Science Center in Seattle. He feels that rats aren't focused enough to learn until they are four months old. The rats trained to play basketball at Ohio's Center of Science and Industry (COSI) begin their training at six to eight weeks of age, and that seems to be about the average. But I have successfully trained rats who were over one year of age. It seems it is almost never too early or too late to train a rat.

## MOTIVATION AND REINFORCERS

Before you start teaching your rat a trick, you must decide what reward to use. As explained in Chapter 3, food is the most common reward or reinforcer used when teaching tricks to an animal. You want to pick a food that your rat likes a lot so that he will be highly motivated to try to earn it. You also want to

use very small pieces for two reasons. First, you want the rat to be able to eat the treat quickly so that you can get back to training. You also want to be able to give him a large number of rewards before he becomes full or tired of the treat.

After experimenting with sunflower seeds and ground nuts, I have decided the easiest and best food to use when training rats is cocoa-flavored rice cereal. Some rats will work for plain cereal, but flavored varieties seem to be more highly motivating for most rats. The trainers at COSI use toasted-oat cereal cut into quarters.

There are other motivators that can be used for rewards. Some rats are so people-oriented and bonded to their human that they want to be wherever you are. In some cases, this desire to be with you is stronger than their desire for food. You can use this type of motivator to teach a trick such as jumping. By placing your rat on one stool and positioning yourself at the far side of a second stool, you can encourage him to jump. It is also often easy to teach this type of rat to jump from the stool to your shoulder. But it will be much harder to teach him to jump back the other way! Some rats may also respond to being petted or praised. For instance, if your rat learns that you will say "Good boy" and pet him when he jumps from one stool to another, this may be all the motivation he needs to do the trick.

Curiosity can also be used to teach tricks. It is a good motivator for tricks such as an obstacle course or rope climb in which your rat will get to do or see something new. Once the novelty wears off, he may or may not continue to perform the trick, depending on his personality.

There are some tricks that will always be easier to teach with food. One of these is the basket pull-up. It is difficult to get a rat interested in pulling up the string to raise the basket unless he knows that there is food in the basket.

## FOCUS AND DISTRACTIONS

The best time of day to train your rat is when he is used to being awake and active. For most rats, this will be first thing in the morning and late afternoon or evening. It's also important to choose a time when you are not tired, irritated, or rushed. Training takes a lot of patience, so you need to be relaxed and rested to be a good trainer.

If you want your rat to perform in public, you will need to have him practice at different times of the day once he has mastered some tricks. Most opportunities for public performances, such as pet fairs, presentations to schools, and television shows, occur during the middle of the day. Working with him at this time of the day will prepare him for the real thing.

Initially, the best location in which to train your rat is a place he feels most comfortable, such as the room in which he is used to playing. If you want

## Treats, Praise... or Me?

Zookeeper and trainer Gary Miller uses small pieces of animal crackers to reward his rats during training. Trainer Judy Reavis first used cat food when training her working rat, Rattie, to run cables through school conduits. Later she discovered that Rattie really loved Gummi Bears, especially the green ones, so that became her reward for helping to rewire schools for the Internet.

For an animal stage show presented at the Sacramento Zoo, a rat named Treat loved bananas so much that it only took a week for him to learn complex tricks like coming out of a hole, walking a thick tightrope, and scurrying into another hole. Interestingly, Treat's successor, Mocha, took longer to train because the staff found that she preferred to be with people more than being rewarded with any food they could offer her. It took her about three months to perform tricks reliably!

him to perform in public later, hold training sessions in other rooms of your house and then progress to other locations outside the home environment.

When first beginning training, be sure that there are no unusual events in the area that might provide a distraction. For instance, if your rat is used to the television being on when he is out playing, you can have the television on during the training session. But if your neighbors are having a party and playing unusually loud music, postpone the training session for another time. Once your rat is well along in his training, a neighborhood party might not be a problem and may provide a good opportunity to get your rat used to distractions while performing.

**Before you start teaching your rat a trick, decide what reward to use. Pick a food that your rat likes a lot so that he will be highly motivated to try to earn it.**

In fact, to prepare your rat for public performances, you will need to start providing distractions for him as his training progresses. Invite friends over to watch. First have them stay at the other side of the room, and then gradually have them come closer. Throughout the session, have them gradually make more noise, and provide them with different noisemakers, such as whistles, rattles, etc. Bring in extra lights to make the room brighter.

## Attention Span

A training session for each rat should only be about 5 to 15 minutes long. While rats do have the ability to repeat an activity many times in a row, they have a short attention span and can be expected to focus for only short periods. Learning a trick is harder and takes more concentration than performing a well-learned task. A trained rat will be able to concentrate for longer periods, but even the highly trained landmine-detection rats mentioned in Chapter 2 are asked to work for only 30 minutes a day out in the field. Rats who are trained to sniff tuberculosis samples are asked to work for only 20 minutes at a time twice a day.

To speed up training, you can hold more than one training session a day. In fact, you could probably hold as many as four training sessions per day as long as you give your rat a break of at least two hours between sessions.

## CHOOSING A TRAINING METHOD

You will find a wide variety of tricks and games listed in Chapters 6 through 9, and the instructions tell the best way of teaching each one. If you invent a new trick, you must decide what method of training you will use based on what would work best: shaping, molding, leading, or targeting. (If you succeed in teaching your rat a new trick that isn't in this book, please let me know!)

# Training Tips

*   Give your rat lots of different experiences to broaden his socialization and increase his intelligence.
*   For trick training, choose a rat who is well socialized, outgoing, and strongly bonded to you.
*   Teach active rats active tricks and lazy rats passive tricks.
*   Begin training in a quiet, familiar area. Later, to prepare your rat for public performances, have him practice in other locations and introduce distractions.
*   Keep training sessions short—only 5 to 15 minutes per session.
*   Hold training sessions at the same time of day every day when you first begin training. Later, have your rat perform at different times of the day to prepare him for public appearances..
*   Choose a reward your rat likes. If he does not seem interested in learning a trick, try a different reward.
*   Be generous with rewards when you begin training. When your rat knows the trick well, occasionally skip the reward to strengthen the behavior, but always end the session on a positive note with a reward.
*   Make sure that your rat is always rewarded immediately after he performs the desired behavior.
*   Choose the cue and method of teaching according to the trick.

# Chapter 6

# Introductory Tricks

The first four tricks presented in this chapter are the easiest ones for most rats to learn, so they are good ones with which to begin training. Once a rat starts to understand what you want him to do and he begins to understand the learning process, it will be easier to teach him more complicated tricks. The other tricks in this chapter are also fairly easy to teach to most rats.

## STAND UP

Stand up is one of the easiest tricks to teach because standing on the hind legs is a natural behavior for a rat. For this trick, all you need are some treats.

- Show your rat the treat, and hold it slightly above his head.
- Give the command "Up," and lift the treat slowly so that your rat will follow it as it moves higher. At first, reward him for any attempt to stand up, and then require that he do it a little better with each attempt.
- Hold the treat higher and higher until your rat is standing up tall.

When your rat seems to understand this trick, you can stop using the treat as a lure and just hold your finger above his head as a cue. Then you can gradually hold your finger farther away so that you can cue him by just pointing above his head.

## KISS

For this trick, you will need a bit of soft food such as yogurt or baby food and some treats.

- Start by putting a bit of soft food on your lip or cheek, and let your rat lick it off. As soon as he does, give him a treat and praise him.
- Give the command "Give me a kiss" or just "Kiss," and repeat the first step.
- Gradually put less and less food on your face, but continue to reward your rat with a treat for licking or touching your lip or cheek. The addition of using a signal such as tapping your finger to your face might help your rat learn this trick more easily.

**The easiest trick to teach a rat is standing on his hind legs, which is a natural behavior for him.**

## TURNING CIRCLES

For this trick, all you need are treats.

- First, show your rat the treat.
- Now begin to move the treat, and use it to lead your rat in a circle. As soon as he has turned a complete circle, give him the food and praise him. You can use a voice command if you like, but a hand signal is the best cue. It works particularly well because the motion helps start your rat off.
- As he begins to get the idea of turning to follow the food, gradually hold your hand up higher and farther away from him.
- As long as your rat continues to make the circle, you can start abbreviating the hand motion until eventually you'll signal your rat to turn just by moving your hand briefly to the right or left.

Just don't practice this trick so much that your rat gets dizzy!

## BASKET PULL-UP

For this trick, you'll need a tiny basket, some string, a platform (table, stool, cardboard box), and tape or a safety pin. You can search for a basket at a craft store or make a simple one with a small paper cup and some twist ties.

- To make a basket from the paper cup, cut it down so it is only about 1 inch (2.5 cm) high.
- Make a handle for this basket with a twist tie, poking the ends through two small holes on each side.
- Tie one end of a 10-inch (25.4-cm) piece of string to the handle of the basket.
- Fasten the other end of the string to the top of a platform such as a stool, table, the top of your rat's cage, or a cardboard box so that it hangs down over the edge of the platform. You can tape the string in place or tie it to a small safety pin.

Before starting the training, be sure that the

platform your rat will be using has good footing—you don't want him to slip and fall while pulling on the string. You can cover a slippery surface with a rug or a rubber bath mat. The best platform will have sides that are flush with the top, like a cardboard box. However, cardboard tends to be slippery and must be covered. If you use a table or stool, the basket will have a tendency to get caught on the edge, tipping and dumping out the treat. This just means you will have to give your rat a treat by hand for successfully pulling up the basket.

Now you are ready to begin teaching the trick:

- Put a treat in the basket and show it to your rat. Let him take several treats out of the basket until he expects the basket to always contain a treat.
- Next, hold the basket down over the edge of the platform so that he has to reach down to take the treat out of it.
- Hold the basket slightly lower each time. Eventually, your rat will no longer be able to reach the treat. He will have a tendency to try to grab the basket with his teeth or hand to pull it up; encourage him to do so. Let him eat the treat out of the basket after he pulls the basket up.
- At this point you can start giving your rat the command "Pull it up." When the basket is too low for your rat to reach it anymore, encourage him to grab the string instead by holding the string and guiding it toward your rat. You may need to pull on the string yourself

## Are You Talking to Me?

Rats have a wide variety of survival skills, and because they are very social animals, they have developed ways to communicate with each other through body language. Your rat will also use the same body language to communicate with you. For example, when waking up, a rat will often stretch and yawn, extending one or both arms. But a rat may also use a yawn to greet people.

When you are holding your rat and he wants you to take him somewhere, he will signal this to you by pointing with his nose. He may first stare intently in one direction, turn to look at you, and then go back to staring again. Or he might bob his head in the direction he wants to go.

A rat who is playful and excited will show you this with a "play dance"—funny twisting movements and jumps—and may run around in circles. You should take this as an invitation to play by using your hand to chase him, pounce on him, tickle him, or wrestle with him gently.

**The basket pull-up. Make sure that the platform your rat will be using for this trick has good footing—you don't want him to slip and fall while pulling on the string.**

to show your rat how to do it. You may also need to hold the basket up for him to get the treat after a good try to reward his efforts, even if he doesn't manage to get the basket all the way up.

- The first time he grabs the string, give him a lot of praise and two or three treats. It won't be long now for him to realize that pulling on the string brings the basket up. Once he does, it will just take some practice for him to learn the best technique for pulling up the string.

Eventually, your rat will be a champion basket puller.

## ACROBATIC TRICKS

Because rats are so athletic and active, it can be easier to teach most of them active tricks than tricks that require them to hold still. The tightrope and the rope climb are among the easiest athletic tricks to teach rats.

### Tightrope Walk

For this trick, you will need some treats, some tape, pillows or a blanket, and two chairs and a wooden dowel or a table and some thick rope. You can try to set up a tightrope by tying a thick rope between two table legs and taping it in place, but it's hard to get the rope really taut. It is much easier to make a tightrope with a wooden dowel and two chairs. A 1/2-inch (1.27-cm) dowel is fairly easy for rats to walk on, while a 3/8-inch (0.97-cm) dowel is more challenging. Or you can use a stiff rope toy for birds designed to hold its shape. The tightrope should be 25 to 30 inches (63.5 to 76.3 cm) long.

- To begin, arrange the chairs so that the seats are 3 inches (7.6 cm) apart. The chairs can either be side by side or facing each other.
- Place the tightrope across the chair seats. Tape 4 to 6 inches (10.2 to 15.2 cm) of one end securely to one chair to keep the tightrope from

rolling. The opposite end of the tightrope should rest freely across the seat of the other chair.

- Put pillows or a large folded blanket underneath the tightrope in case your rat falls.
- Place your rat on the chair the tightrope is taped to, and give him a few treats so that he feels comfortable there.
- Lead your rat from one chair to the other by having him follow the treat. With the chairs this close, he will only need to use the tightrope for a few steps. When he successfully arrives at the other end, give him the treat.
- Gradually move the free chair farther away, 1/4 inch (0.64 cm) at a time, so that your rat will gradually have to walk farther and farther on the tightrope. Do not move the chair when your rat is on it because that might scare him.

A tightrope 15 inches (38.1 cm) long or longer will make an impressive trick. Your rat will need to learn both skill and self-confidence in balancing on the tightrope, so don't rush the training process. Let him learn at his own pace.

The tightrope walk. Because rats are so athletic and energetic, it can be easier to teach them active tricks rather than tricks that require them to hold still.

### The Rope Climb

For this trick, you will need treats, a table, a length of thick rope, some heavy string, and tape.

- Cut a thick cotton, sisal, or other natural fiber rope 1 foot (30.5 cm) longer than the height of the table. (Later you can switch to a thinner rope, but don't use anything thinner than No. 21 seine twine.)
- Next, run a piece of heavy string across the top of the table, underneath it, and back around to the top. Tighten and tie both ends securely.
- Take one end of the heavy rope and tie it to the string so that the rope hangs down from the edge of the table to the floor. You may need to tape the string to the table to hold it in place.
- Place a heavy object like a brick or a book on the opposite end of the rope now sitting on the floor to hold it taut. (Or instead of the rope, you can use the stiff rope toy for birds mentioned in the previous trick.)

Now that you are set up, you are ready to begin training:

- Set your rat on the book or brick platform, and hold the treat above his head next to the rope. You want your rat to stand on his hind legs to reach for the treat. He should grab onto the rope for support, and as soon as he does, give him the treat.

# A Rat's Tail

One reason many people dislike rats is because of their naked tail. It reminds them of a snake or worm. A rat's tail isn't really naked, though; it's covered with sparse, bristly hairs. These hairs can help keep a rat from slipping backward when climbing. However, the main function of the tail is to help maintain balance. For instance, as your rat walks the tightrope in a trick, he might fling his tail from side to side to keep himself from falling off, or he may even wrap it around the tightrope for added security.

Another main function of the rat's tail is temperature regulation. Rats do not sweat or pant to cool themselves. Instead, a hot rat will circulate extra blood to the surface of his tail to radiate away body heat. The only time a rat's tail will feel warm is when he is overheated. Some fancy rats are bred to be tailless, much like Manx cats, and these individuals are at a disadvantage. Not only are they less adept at climbing and jumping, but they must be kept at temperatures below 80°F (26.7°C) to prevent heatstroke.

- Next, hold the treat a little bit higher and try to get him to start climbing the rope. Continue to reward your rat whenever he grabs onto the rope, and each time hold the treat a little higher.
- Your rat should catch on fairly quickly and start to climb the rope. The first time he does so, give him the treat immediately along with lots of praise.
- The next time, make him climb 1 inch (2.5 cm) or so before getting the treat. At first he may drop off the rope to eat. That's okay. Before long, he'll cling to the rope while chewing the small treat and be ready to continue to climb.

Gradually ask him to climb higher and higher before giving him the treat. Eventually, he will be willing to climb all the way to the top before he gets his reward.

## INSIDE BARREL ROLL

You will need a special prop for this trick, a "barrel" about 1 foot (30.5 cm) in diameter. You can use an exercise wheel taken off its support or a section cut from a 5-gallon (18.9-liter) bucket or other round storage container. It should be 6 to 8 inches (15.2 to 20.3 cm) wide. You can decorate the outside of the barrel with fabric, paint, glitter, sequins, etc.

It will be easier to teach your rat this trick if he already knows how to use an exercise wheel. Getting inside the barrel and making it roll by walking along inside of it is basically the same behavior as walking inside an exercise wheel. You must either teach this trick on the floor or on a table that has barriers around all the edges. Make sure that the barrel does not fall off the table with your rat in it at all costs! You can make barriers at the edge of a table easily enough by using rolled-up towels.

- Show your rat the barrel, which is lying on its side. He will probably get right inside of it. When he does, praise him and reward him immediately. If he doesn't, try to lead him inside the barrel with a treat. (At this point, some rats might start the barrel rolling right away. If not, proceed with the following steps.)
- Once your rat is inside the barrel, reward him with praise and a treat for standing upright and facing in the right direction.
- Next, reward him for moving his hand up the side of the barrel and then for taking a step.
- As he gets the barrel rolling, reward him immediately after each successful attempt to move it. Continue this process.

It shouldn't take long for him to get the idea.

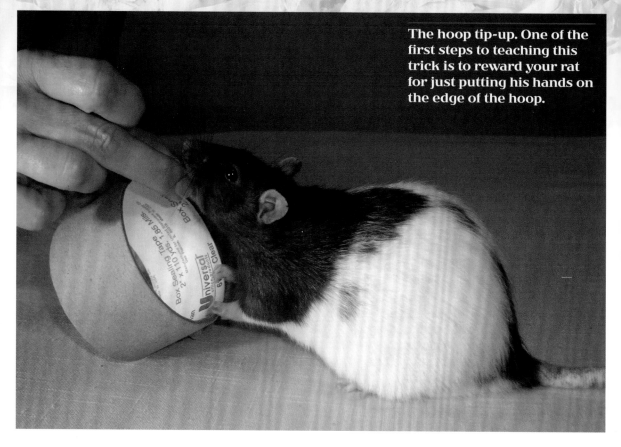

The hoop tip-up. One of the first steps to teaching this trick is to reward your rat for just putting his hands on the edge of the hoop.

## HOOP TIP-UP

For this trick, you will need some treats and three (or more) cardboard hoops. For smaller rats, you can use the cardboard roll from the inside of a roll of packing tape. For larger rats, cut the hoops from a round oatmeal container. Make each hoop 3 inches (7.6 cm) wide so that it will stand when tipped up on its side. The outside of the hoops can be decorated.

- First, teach your rat to go through one hoop by leading him through with a treat. Then teach your rat to go through three hoops in a row.
- Next, lay a hoop flat and show your rat how you can tip it upright by pressing on its edge. Encourage your rat to put his hands on the edge of the hoop and tip it up. Remember to reward him for just touching the hoop at first, and then gradually require that he push harder on the hoop.

Before too long, your rat should understand how to stand the hoop up and then go through it. Then ask him to do the same with the two hoops in a row, then three hoops in a row, etc.

## JUMPING TRICKS

Jumping is another natural behavior for rats, so it tends to be fairly easy to teach. Almost all rats are good jumpers, but some do not have the self-confidence to believe that they can jump.

Teach jumping tricks slowly to give your rat time to learn self-confidence and to develop the necessary muscles. Let him get plenty of practice jumping short distances at first, to build up both his self-confidence and muscles. Don't ask your rat to jump too much in one day, or he might get too tired to enjoy it.

### The Platform Jump

As with the tightrope trick, put a pillow or thickly folded blanket underneath the jumping platforms for padding in case your rat falls.

Most rats can learn to jump a distance of at least 1 foot (30.5 cm), and some athletic rats can jump much farther. Set up two stable platforms about the same height. You can use two chairs or stools, a footstool and a couch, or a chair and a bed, for instance. Make sure that the platforms are sturdy and their surfaces have good footing. The surface of a varnished wood chair will be too slippery, so you can cover it with a rubber bath mat. If you plan to teach your rat to walk a tightrope, you should probably teach that trick first. If your rat learns to jump first, he may jump rather than learn the tightrope.

- Start with the platforms as close together as possible.
- Lead your rat from one platform to the other with a treat.
- Slowly spread the platforms apart, 1/4 inch (0.64) at a time. Never move the platform on which your rat is standing. This will scare him and discourage him from jumping.
- When the platforms are 3 inches (7.6 cm) apart, instead of leading him across, hold the treat on the other side, tap the platform with your finger, say his name, and then give the command "Jump." At first he will be able to just walk over the gap, but as it widens, he will eventually have to take the plunge and jump across. When he makes his first jump, shower him with treats and praise.

How fast you'll be able to widen the gap will depend on your rat's personality and how motivated he is to get the treat. It's best if you widen the gap as slowly as possible.

Once your rat has learned to jump, you can expand on the idea for all kinds of creative tricks. For instance, you can sit on the far platform and ask your rat to jump to your lap. Be sure to wear clothing that covers your legs so that you don't get scratched.

# First-Rate Jumpers

Rats are quite athletic and can jump a long distance compared to their body length. Some rats can jump up to 4 feet (1.2 m) from a standing start, which is more than four times their body length. Compare that to the human record of just over 12 feet (3.7 m) for the standing broad jump. Rats can even perform such feats in near darkness. How can they do it? There is evidence that rats can use ultrasounds for a simple type of echolocation, much in the way bats do.

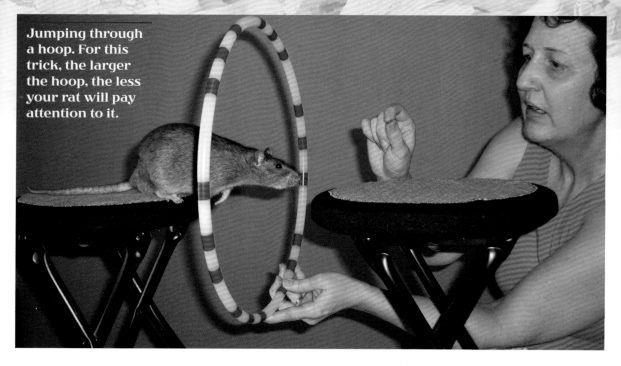

Jumping through a hoop. For this trick, the larger the hoop, the less your rat will pay attention to it.

### Jumping to Your Shoulder

You teach this trick the same way you teach platform jumping, except you use your shoulder as the second platform.

- Sit or stand so that your shoulder is at about the same height as the platform from which your rat is jumping. Begin with your shoulder next to the platform.
- Now tap your shoulder to get your rat to climb onto it.
- Gradually move farther away until your rat is jumping to your shoulder.

You can also try to teach your rat to jump from your shoulder to the platform, but most rats would rather jump to their person rather than away from her.

### Jumping Through a Hoop

There are two ways to teach this trick: the easy way and the hard way. In fact, the easy way doesn't really require much training.

Once your rat knows the platform jump, you can hold an embroidery hoop centered between two platforms and he will probably jump right through it. A hoop at least 1 foot (30.5 cm) across is large enough that most rats won't pay it much notice. However, hold it at least 5 inches (12.7 cm) away from the platform your rat is standing on because if it is any closer, he might try to step onto it. You can dress up this trick by gluing paper tongues of fire to the top of the hoop!

The second way to teach your rat to jump through a hoop is to have him perform it on a solid surface instead of using platforms. It is much more difficult to teach your rat to jump though a hoop this way because he will want to scramble through it rather than actually jump through it. It might help if you teach him to jump through the hoop with the platforms first.

This trick must be performed on a nonslip surface, such as a table covered with a blanket.

- Lead your rat through the hoop with a treat several times.
- Continue to lead your rat through the hoop, holding it a little higher each time.
- When the hoop is high enough, your rat will probably try to go under the hoop instead of through it. Gently put him back to the beginning and tell him "Jump." Lower the hoop if necessary.
- When the hoop is too high for your rat to step through, he will probably want to scramble over it rather than jump over it. Encourage him to jump by getting really excited when you give the command "Jump." Snapping your fingers on the opposite side of the hoop might also stimulate him to jump. Lifting your rat through the hoop might also help give him the right idea.
- Continue to practice in this manner, and treat and praise your rat for every step in the right direction.

# Exercise Wheels

Regular exercise is necessary for your rat's health and longevity. While it is important to let your pet out of his cage every day for playtime, he will likely spend the majority of his time in it. One of the best ways to ensure that he gets enough exercise is to supply him with an exercise wheel in his enclosure. Most rats will learn to use a wheel if they are given the chance to play with one as youngsters.

A rat wheel must be at least 10 inches (25.4 cm) in diameter; larger wheels are necessary for big males. Even smaller rats prefer running on a larger wheel. Wheels with solid running surfaces or those made of 1/4 inch (0.64 cm) square mesh are safer than those made of metal bars because they remove the risk of a rat getting his feet or tail caught.

# Chapter 7
# Advanced Tricks

**I**f you have a rat who likes to perform tricks, here is a selection that takes more time and patience to teach than those in the previous chapter.

## PASSIVE TRICKS

Passive tricks can be very easy to teach some rats, while others just hate to hold still for too long. Once a rat learns how to stay on command, though, you can get him to sit almost anywhere for a variety of tricks.

### Stay

To teach the stay trick, you will need treats and a large coffee can.
- Stand a large coffee can on its end.
- Place your rat on top of the can and gently press him in place, giving the command "Stay." You can also hold the palm of your hand in front of him as a visual signal.
- At first, give him a treat right away. Then gradually require that he stay in place for longer periods, up to one minute.
- Once he will stay on the can, practice asking him to stay on a table.
- Continue to practice this until he no longer requires the treats to stay in place.

This trick will take a fair amount of practice for most rats.

### Ride on a Moving Vehicle

Once your rat knows how to stay, you can have him ride on or in a variety of rat-sized vehicles, including cars, trucks, motorcycles, scooters, baby carriages, wagons, etc. You can also have your rat sit on toy horses, as long as they are stable (no pun intended!). To find such vehicles, you can try looking in toy stores, dollar stores, craft stores, discount or closeout stores, and thrift stores.

You will start with the same techniques used for the stay and build on it to gradually add motion. You can either pull or push the vehicle across the table yourself, or you can set up a ramp for the vehicle to roll down. Use a board at least 2 feet (5.1 cm) long and an object about 1 to 2 inches (2.5 to 5.1 cm) thick, such as a book, under one end of the ramp to

**The stay. Teaching your rat to stay is much easier when he is up on a platform.**

make the incline. Place a thin sheet of cardboard at the bottom of the ramp to minimize the bump from the board to the table.

- Once your rat will remain seated in the vehicle, move it forward a few inches (several cm). Praise him for sitting still and give him a treat.
- Gradually move the vehicle a greater and greater distance before rewarding him.
- If using the ramp, place the vehicle near the bottom of the ramp and let it roll down a few inches (several cm). When your rat is used to that and will sit still for his treat, gradually place the vehicle higher up on the ramp so that it will roll farther each time. Continue to praise and reward your rat for each successful roll.

If your rat really seems to like riding in a vehicle, you can even train him to ride in a remote control car. Jeeps made for dolls are about the right size. Be very careful when operating these cars because some of them have a tendency to accelerate quickly at the start, which might cause your rat to fall off.

## Balance an Object on the Head

For a rat who knows how to stay, this trick should be quickly learned. You might try using a thimble, a small spool, a Popsicle stick, or other similar items.

- Simply tell your rat "Stay," and then place the item on his head.
- At first, leave it on his head for only a second, then remove it and reward your rat with a treat.
- Gradually let the item stay on his head longer and longer. Don't give him the treat until you remove the object because it will likely fall when he takes the treat.
- Your rat has successfully learned the trick when he will hold the item on his head for at least five seconds.

If your rat is really good at balancing an item on his head, you might see if he can walk with it on there. One of my Rat Fan Club members once taught her rat to jump from one platform to another with a Popsicle stick balanced on his head!

## Play Dead

This is a very difficult trick to teach rats because the only time they normally lie on their side is when they are sleeping.

- Begin by gently pushing your rat into a lying position on his stomach. The cutest command to use for this trick is "Bang!" (as if you are shooting him with a toy gun).
- Gradually push your rat over onto his side more and more as you try to shape this trick.
- At first, give him the treat as soon as he is in the position you want. Then, as you practice, require that he stay in that position longer and longer for up to five seconds.
- The trick is complete when he will lie on his side for five seconds.

## Lie on the Back

This is the ultimate in passive tricks. A rat has to have complete trust in you to lie on his back in your hand.

- Begin by holding your rat sitting up on your chest, and give him a favorite treat.
- Gradually lean him farther and farther back into your hand, stopping if he shows any sign of being uncomfortable. Give him a treat each time you lean him back farther.

# Talking It Over

I try to talk to my rats as much as possible, and I do think that they understand a lot more than most people might expect. It seems the more you talk to them, the more they learn to understand you. Try telling them what is going to happen; it can't hurt, and the verbal communication might help make them feel more comfortable and secure. For instance, if you have to do a medical procedure, such as cleaning out an infected ear, describe what you need to do, explain that it might be uncomfortable now but it will make your rattie feel better soon, and ask him to be patient and hold still. I usually get better cooperation from my rats when I do this. If you want one of your rats to pose for a photograph, ask him to hold still so that you can take his picture to show people how handsome he is. Or if you are going out of town, tell your rats how long you'll be gone and when you'll be back, and explain who will care for them while you're away. If you develop the habit of chatting to your rats on a regular basis, you will build a stronger relationship with them.

Once your rat learns how to sit still in a toy vehicle, you can work on teaching him to stay while you push or pull it slowly.

•   Use lots of praise to encourage him to stay on his back.
Rats with a laid-back personality will be more likely to do this trick.

## MINOR MOVEMENT TRICKS

It helps if your rat already knows how to stay before you teach him minor movement tricks. Using a prop such as a "podium" or placing your rat on top of a large coffee can help him stay in one place. It may also be helpful to use clicker training when teaching these tricks so that you can let your rat know immediately when he has done the behavior you want.

### Wave

It is easiest to teach the wave trick if you first teach your rat to stand with his hands on an object such as a short, heavy glass turned upside down, which serves as a sort of "podium."

- First, teach your rat to stand at the podium by leading him into position with a treat. As you lift the treat over your rat's head, he is likely to put his hands on the podium naturally for support. Praise him and give him the treat.
- Repeat this until he understands that you want him to keep his hands on the podium. You might use the command "Place."
- Once your rat is standing up at the podium, hold a treat in front of him just out of his reach, and encourage him to reach for it with one of his hands.
- As soon as he lifts his hand, give him the treat.
- Continue to shape this behavior by repeating the exercise until your rat is consistently lifting one hand. For a good wave, encourage him to lift his hand up high two or three times. Use the command "Wave."

Once your rat knows how to stand at the podium, you can also use clicker training to teach him to wave.

- First, train him to recognize the clicker as a secondary reinforcer. (See Chapter 3.)

**Shake hands. This trick is similar to the wave, except instead of just lifting his hand, you now want your rat to put it on your finger.**

- With your rat standing at the podium, watch for any movement of either of his hands. As soon as you see one of his hands move, no matter how small the movement, click and give him a treat. This is now the hand that you will train your rat to wave.
- Wait for your rat to move this hand again, then click and reward. Continue clicking and rewarding any small movements of this hand only.
- When your rat is habitually making movements of his hand, begin reinforcing only movements of his hand in an upward direction.
- Once your rat is habitually making upward movements of his hand, wait until he moves his hand higher before clicking and giving him the treat. Continue doing this for each movement higher and higher.
- When your rat is habitually moving his hand up into a waving position, require that he make two movements of his hand before reinforcing him. Then require three hand movements, etc.
- When your rat consistently waves his hand up and down three times, he has successfully learned the trick.

### Shake Hands

Because rats are so short, this trick is more visible if you teach it like the wave—by using a "podium." This time, instead of teaching your rat to just lift his hand, you want him to put his hand on your finger.

- Hold the treat so that it is close to one of your rat's hands. Because rats can be either right- or left-handed, you'll have to see which hand he prefers using.
- To start, reward him for either lifting his hand or touching your fingers. Then, just reward him for touching your finger. At first, you can hold the treat between your finger and thumb, but once he is touching your finger, stop holding the treat in that hand and offer just your finger.
- Once he is consistently putting his hand on your finger, you can start gently moving your finger up and down. At first, move your finger only a little, then gradually move it a little more until you are "shaking" his hand.

Because this trick just asks your rat to respond to your signal (holding out your finger), it is fairly easy to teach.

### Drink From the Hand

This is a cute trick that some rats will even do on their own! Use a small, heavy crock or pet dish that won't tip over.

- Fill the dish almost to the top with apple juice and place it next to your rat.

## Using a Clicker

When using a clicker with your rat, you must be careful to choose one that isn't too loud because the clicking sound may scare him. In fact, when I first start clicker training a rat, I hold the clicker behind my back to muffle the sound. Once he starts to associate the sound with the food, I then slowly move my hand closer until I can hold the clicker in a comfortable position.

- Give him the command "Take a drink," then gently dip his hand in the juice and let it go. His natural inclination will be to lick the juice off.
- Praise him and give him a treat.
- Repeat this procedure until he begins to put his hand in the juice himself.

Keep in mind that equal numbers of rats are either right- or left-handed, so if he doesn't seem to want to use one hand, try the other.

**Walk on hind legs/dance.** Once your rat is able to walk on his hind legs, you can teach him to dance.

## Shake the Head

Although the steps for shake the head are very simple, this trick takes a lot of repetition to learn.

- Gently touch or tickle your rat's ear, or blow in his ear to try to get him to shake his head.
- When he does, immediately praise him and give him a treat. If you are using a clicker, click immediately when he shakes his head.

Rather than using a command like "Shake," it can be cute to say "Am I right?" or something similar.

## Nod

Also a simple trick, the nod trick can be used to simply charm your audience.

- Hold the treat in front of your rat and move it up and down so that his head follows the movement of the treat. One command you can use is "Do you love me?"
- At first, make your rat only nod once before giving him the treat. Then make him nod at least two or three times before rewarding him.

As your rat starts to get the idea, you can move your hand farther away, still making the up and down movement.

## ACTIVE TRICKS

Because most rats tend to be fairly active, these types of tricks are easier to teach than passive tricks. Not only are they fun for your rat, for you, and for any potential audience, but they also provide him with good exercise.

### Walk on Hind Legs

While teaching a rat to stand on his hind legs is easy, it's much harder to get a rat to walk on his hind legs. It helps if you teach him to stand up first. (See Chapter 6.) You'll need a surface that has good traction, such as a blanket spread across the top of a table, and of course some treats.

- Hold a treat above your rat's head.
- When he stands up, move your hand forward to encourage him to walk forward.
- At first, reward him with a treat each time he takes a step. He will probably drop down on all fours to eat it; if so, you will need to start over each time.
- Gradually require your rat to walk a little farther before giving him the treat.
- Some rats may be willing to take up to five steps, while others may be willing to travel farther.

This trick must be taught in slow steps to give your rat a chance to build up the muscles needed.

### Dance

This trick is similar to walking on hind legs, but instead of asking your rat to walk, you are going to ask him to turn in circles. Once again, it helps if your rat knows how to stand up first.

- Hold the treat above your rat's head.
- Slowly move the treat in a small circle above his head to encourage him to turn in a circle.
- At first, reward him for turning only a short way. As in the previous trick, he will probably drop down to eat the treat, so you will need to start over each time.
- Gradually require him to turn a little farther before giving him the treat until he will turn at least one full circle.

### Barrel Roll

The barrel roll is difficult to teach, and it takes a lot of practice. You'll need a 6- to 8-inch (15.2- to 20.3-cm) section cut from a 5-gallon (18.9-l) plastic bucket for the barrel. (You can use the same prop for the inside barrel-roll trick taught in Chapter 6.)

- Place a blanket on a table. Lay the barrel on its side on the blanket with the open end facing your nondominant hand. The blanket will

The barrel roll. This is a difficult trick to teach, but it will impress audiences. If you give your rat the treat every time he takes a small step, he'll eventually learn to roll the barrel.

help keep the barrel from rolling too fast.
- Put your nondominant hand inside the barrel to hold it steady and to control how fast it rolls.

There are two ways to teach this trick: leading or shaping.

## Leading Method

For the leading method:
- Hold a treat in your dominant hand and put your rat on top of the barrel.
- Give him a few treats while he sits on the barrel so that he learns that he will be rewarded for being on it.
- Hold the treat in front of your rat to encourage him to take a step while you allow the barrel to roll backward slightly.
- Give the command "Roll it."
- At first, give your rat the treat every time he takes a small step.

Gradually require that he take two steps, then three steps, etc., before he gets the treat. With enough practice, your rat will learn to roll the barrel.

### Shaping Method

For the shaping method, you will probably want to use clicker training. You will need to hold the barrel steady with the same hand in which you hold the clicker so that you can deliver treats with your dominant hand.

- Put your rat on the barrel and give him a few treats.
- Wait for him to move any of his feet. As soon as he does, click and give him a treat.
- Gradually require that he move another one of his feet before you click and reward him; this will encourage him to take a step. Then make him actually take a step before you click and reward him.
- After he takes one full step, require that he take more and more steps forward before you click and reward him.
- Once your rat is walking steadily forward, the shaping process is finished.

## Roll Over

This is a very difficult trick to teach rats. Rolling over is not a natural behavior for them the way it is for dogs. Some rats might learn this trick more easily if you teach them to play dead first. (See "Play Dead.") A more natural way to teach this trick is to use the rat's tendency to turn over on his back

# By a Whisker

A rat's whiskers are very sensitive. He uses them to sense his environment during his wanderings. Whiskers near the eyes, lips, and cheeks perceive horizontal and ground surfaces, while the ones above the eyes detect overhead surfaces. They are so acutely sensitive that a rat can use them to tell the difference between a rough wall and a smooth wall. In fact, a rat can be trained to tell the difference between sandpaper with 200 grains per cubic centimeter and 25 grains per cubic centimeter.

Studies have shown that whiskers of different lengths vibrate at a different frequency, helping a rat build up an image of the environment in his brain. And the whiskers are not just passive sensory organs—a rat actively whisks them back and forth to detect the shape and texture of objects in his path. A rat can extend his whiskers out in front of him up to 2 inches (5.1 cm). The whiskers even help a rat detect slight air movements and water currents when he is swimming.

when he is wrestling with another rat. Very trusting rats will do this when playing with a person, although many won't.

- When you can get your rat to lie down or turn on his back, show him that you have a treat and encourage him to roll over by moving the treat around his head. Use the command "Over."
- Once he starts to get the idea, you can try the trick with your rat starting in a standing position.
- Hold the treat in front of your rat, and move it around behind his head.
- Encourage him to lie down by gently pressing on him with your wrist. Then follow the previous sequence.

With enough practice, your rat may roll over on command.

## RETRIEVING TRICKS

Retrieving is the basis for several other tricks that require your rat to carry something in his mouth. Using a clicker makes it much easier to teach retrieving tricks. Before teaching fetch, review the clicker training section in Chapter 3. Once your rat understands that the click sound means that a treat is coming and he responds to it reliably, you can start teaching him to retrieve.

### Fetch/Retrieve

Choose an item you want your rat to fetch. A crumpled ball of paper about 1/2 inch (1.27 cm) in diameter, a strip of rag tied in a knot, or a twig works well.

- Put the fetch item down next to your rat and be ready to click and reward him for sniffing the object. If he doesn't show any interest in the item, try a different item or put a dab of food on the object.
- Click and reward your rat for sniffing or touching the object with his nose several times, then stop clicking to encourage him to try new behaviors. When your rat starts touching the object with his teeth, click and reward again. If he has no tendency to touch the object with his teeth, put a dab of food on the object.
- Next, stop clicking to encourage your rat to pick the object up. When he picks the object up, click and reward again. Now you can start using the command "Fetch."
- Once your rat is picking up the object consistently, call him to come before clicking, and reward him for bringing the object to you. If he drops the object before coming, do not reward him.
- Give the command "Fetch" again, and redirect his attention to the object by pointing to it or touching it, and reward him for picking it up again.
- Then gradually require that he hold the object in his mouth for longer

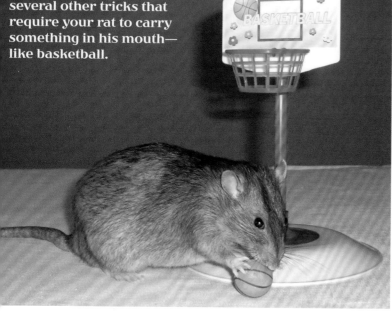

**Retrieving is the basis for several other tricks that require your rat to carry something in his mouth— like basketball.**

periods of time. Once he is holding the object for a few seconds, try calling him to you again.

• When he is coming to you with the object consistently, hold out your hand and reward him for dropping the object into your hand.

Once your rat is retrieving the stationary object, you can start tossing it a short distance. Gradually increase the distance your rat has to run after the object, and you will have a full retrieve.

## Basketball

You teach the basketball trick basically the same way you teach fetch. For a basketball prop, you can use a crumpled piece of paper or an orange Wiffle ball. You'll find instructions for making a basketball hoop in Chapter 10.

I visited the Center of Science and Industry (COSI) in Cincinnati, Ohio, to see how they train their rats to play basketball. I learned that it can take several months before rats reliably perform this trick. Each rat is trained five times a day, with the trainer asking him to make about 15 baskets each session. Liz, a trainer there, said that most people do not understand how much time is actually involved in training rats.

The COSI rats are first trained to associate the sound of an electronic buzzer with the treat. The treat is toasted-oat cereal cut into quarters. The rats get their treat from a little window in the wall of the basketball court. Each rat is first taught to pick up the ball and carry it to the treat window. Later, the rats are taught to carry the ball to the basket. Because the baskets are attached to the wall of the court, they cannot be lowered, so the rats are taught to climb on a platform to put the ball into the basket. Gradually, the platform is lowered and then eventually removed. I think that it is easier to use a basket that can be lowered and raised.

Using a clicker, you can train your rat in small steps to pick up the ball, carry it to the basket, and then put it in the basket.

• First, teach your rat to pick up the ball using the same steps used to teach the retrieve. (See "Fetch/Retrieve.") Once your rat is consistently picking up the ball, place it near the basket. Start with the basket in its lowest position.

- Now when your rat picks up the ball, don't click and reward him until he makes a small movement toward the basket.
- After you give your rat a treat, wait for him to pick up the ball again, then wait for him to move toward the basket before you click and reward him. Gradually require that he move closer and closer to the basket with the ball before you click and reward him.
- When your rat reaches the basket, wait until he moves the ball slightly above the basket before clicking and rewarding him. Gradually require that he hold the ball above the basket before you click and reward him.
- Now wait until your rat moves the ball slightly down inside the basket before you click and reward him. Gradually require that he put the ball farther and farther down inside the basket before clicking and rewarding him. Eventually he will be putting the ball all the way through the basket.

By this time, most rats will be very attached to the ball, and some will not want to release it. They will dive through the basket while still holding the ball in their mouth! Many of the COSI rats do this, and they only stop doing so when they grow too large to go through the basket.

Once your rat is consistently putting the ball through the basket, gradually raise the basket a fraction of an inch (a fraction of a centimeter) at a time to the desired height. When you raise the basket this slowly, your rat will not hesitate to put the ball in the basket each time.

## Basketball Behind the Scenes

The balls that trainers use at the Center of Science and Industry (COSI) for rattie basketball are donated by a deodorant company—they are the small plastic balls (1¼ inches [3.2 cm] in diameter) designed to go inside roll-on deodorant bottles! The trainers at COSI drill several holes into the ball so that the rats can grip it with their teeth as well as with their hands.

When I attended a performance, I was amazed to see how much the rats actually use their hands to put the ball into the hoop. I expected them to use only their teeth, but they lifted the ball with their teeth and then put it through the hoop with their hands.

I was also surprised to learn that rattie basketball players can be rather intimidating athletes. COSI only trains female rats to play basketball to prevent possible aggression between males. However, for the show I saw, they had put a clear plastic divider down the middle of the court because, as the presenter explained, these two particular performing rats did not get along with each other.

### Firefighter Rescue

This is a cute trick in which you teach your rat to climb a ladder to rescue a little doll from a "burning" building and then carry it to an ambulance. If the ambulance is large enough, you can have the rat get into the ambulance with the doll. If not, you can teach your rat to just put the doll into the ambulance. You teach this trick the same way you teach basketball. The hardest part of the trick is finding the rat-sized ambulance, although adding a red cross to a regular toy truck or van works just fine. You can also make an ambulance out

**Firefighter rescue. This trick combines several basic skills your rat can easily learn.**

of a box. A rat-sized ladder truck is a nice touch, but you can also just use a wooden bird ladder attached to a box you paint like a burning building. The box must be weighted down so that it won't tip over.

You need to teach the rat to retrieve the doll first, then teach him to put the doll into the ambulance. Next, you teach the rat to climb the ladder to retrieve the doll and then teach him to put it into the ambulance. You teach your rat to climb the ladder by leading him with a treat. (Follow the steps given in "Retrieve" and "Basketball.")

### Recycling Rats

This trick is based on the recycling rats trained by Gary Miller mentioned in Chapter 5. Gary said that it took about a month to train the rats and another month and a half to fine-tune the show. He trained each rat twice a day for about 15 minutes. Gary used clicker training with each rat in a 20-gallon (75.7 l) aquarium to control their movements and keep their attention on the task.

He started out with a cottage cheese lid as a feeding station. He would click, then put a piece of food on the lid. He continued this until the rat would go to the lid for the food every time the clicker sounded. He then exchanged the lid for a very short piece of PVC pipe that was 3 inches (7.6 cm) in diameter. He gradually switched to taller containers until he reached a height of 3 inches (7.6 cm) tall. The first container was always in the same position in the aquarium, let's say the left front corner.

For the next step, Gary took a little piece of wadded-up paper and put a little peanut butter on it. When the rat picked the paper up in his mouth, he would click. Remember, the rat was still trained to go to the feeding station when he heard the click. Gary said that most of the time the rat would bring the paper with him to the feeding station to get his treat. The rat would then drop the item into the feeding station to pick up the treat. Once that behavior was established, Gary moved on to the next item.

To train the rat to "recycle" metal, he moved the container to the opposite corner of the aquarium and went back to the simple click and feed routine. He observed that it usually didn't take much time for the rat to get used to the new item. Next, he used a bottle cap and put the peanut butter it. He worked on training the rat to take the bottle cap to the container until that behavior was established.

Finally, Gary put the container in the middle of the aquarium and switched the object to a plastic pen cap. Once the rat had learned to take the pen cap to the container in the middle of the aquarium, it was time to try using three containers in the various spots. Gary said that the hard part was to get the rats to differentiate one place from another and to put the right object in the correct container. Of course, it was important for the containers to always be in the same order in the aquarium.

Initially, when the rats retrieved each object and dropped it into the correct container, they were still taking the food reward out of that container. Once the rats were doing this behavior well, Gary started putting the food outside the container. Now the rats would drop the item into the container and then get the food on the floor outside the container. Gary also eventually stopped putting peanut butter on the objects.

Once the rats had learned the entire routine, Gary found that they started taking the objects back out of the containers so that they could put them in again for another reward! To prevent this from getting out of hand, he took modified plastic funnels and attached them to the inside rim of each container. Now when the rats dropped an object into the receptacle, it slid down the funnel and into the container and out of the rat's reach.

For the show's big finish, Gary trained the rats to pull a string that released a banner that said "Please recycle." (For step-by-step instructions to the banner trick, see Chapter 8.)

# Prop Tricks

**A**ll these tricks rely on specific props with which your rat interacts. While some of the previous tricks also need props, they are improvised more easily. The first seven of these tricks are fairly easy to teach.

## SMALL PICNIC BASKET

This is a very simple trick for your rat to learn. It will require a small picnic basket, say 4 to 5 inches (10.2 to 12.7 cm) across, and it should have an attached lid that flips up. You can probably find one in craft stores or thrift shops.

Before beginning the training, stick the basket to the table with double-stick tape.

- To start, place your rat on the table next to the basket. Next, hold the lid open and show your rat that you're putting a treat inside of it.
- Now let your rat reach into the basket to take the treat out.
- Repeat this several times, and then gradually lower the lid more and more. At a certain point, your rat will need to push the lid up slightly to get his nose into the basket to look inside.
- Each successive time, require your rat to push the lid up farther by himself before you offer help. If necessary, encourage him to lift the lid by lifting it slightly with your finger.
- Each time he sticks his head into the basket, he is obviously rewarded with the treat he finds inside of it, which will motivate him to repeat the trick.

Eventually, your rat will learn how to open the lid of the basket to get the treat without needing your help.

## LARGE PICNIC BASKET

This is a more entertaining version of the small basket trick.

The basket trick. Prop tricks rely on specific objects with which your rat interacts.

You need a picnic basket about 18 inches (45.7 cm) long, with a lid that flips up on each side. The lid needs to stick out from the rim a little so that your rat can easily lift it with his nose. If it doesn't, you can glue a little tab on the edge of the lid on one end. You can usually find one of these baskets in a department store or sporting goods store, or you can order one on the Internet.

Basically, you teach this trick the same way you teach the smaller basket trick described earlier, but you get your rat to actually go inside the basket to get the treat. And because you are using a larger basket, you can train your rat to go in one side and come out on the other. It can be more difficult to get him to come back out of the basket, however, especially when he is performing for an audience. But I have found that most people think it's very funny that the rat will go into the basket but won't come out, and they enjoy the trick anyway.

To train the trick, follow the same steps given for the small basket and just add the following:

- To teach your rat to come back out of the basket, open the lid on the

other end of the basket and lead him out with a treat.
- Give him the treat as soon as he is out of the basket.
- Practice this until your rat consistently understands that he will receive a treat each time he exits the basket.

## BALLOON PULL-DOWN

For this trick, you'll need a buoyant helium balloon on a string and a tiny plastic cup (like the disposable ones used for condiments at fast-food restaurants). Be sure that the balloon is quite buoyant or it may not be able to support the weight of the cup. Your rat may learn this trick quicker if you first teach him the basket pull-up trick in Chapter 6.
- Poke a hole in the plastic cup just under the rim. Thread about 20 inches (50.8 cm) of the balloon's string through the hole, and tie a knot so that the cup will hang from the string. Tie the remaining end of the string to a small object heavy enough to anchor the balloon.
- Show your rat the balloon so that he'll get used to it and won't be afraid of it.
- Now show your rat that there are treats in the cup, and let him eat several from it. Gradually hold the cup higher and higher so that he has to stand on his hind legs to eat from it. (There should always be treats in the cup for your rat to eat).
- Eventually, your rat won't be able to reach the cup and will have to

# The Rat in the Hat

Some rats are willing to wear a simple costume, such as a hat and cape, when performing tricks. This can add a great deal of panache to the performance, especially for tricks such as the firefighter's rescue. Look for rat-sized hats at dollar stores and craft stores. Also look for small plush toys in thrift shops that may have hats, scarves, and capes that can be used. You will probably need to attach an elastic band to most hats, which will go under your rat's neck to keep the hat on.

Rats don't like costumes that restrict their movement and so don't like to wear clothing that fits around their arms or legs. However, most rats won't object to wearing a hat as long as the elastic band isn't too tight or too loose. A hat that is too loose can slide down and get in the way of their eyesight or even their arm movement. Most will also accept wearing a scarf or cape, again, as long as it doesn't interfere with their arms.

Beans, the rat who was the model for most of the pictures in this book, can be seen performing the basket pull-up trick wearing a king's crown and cape on a television news video on the Internet. For the link, visit www.ratfanclub.org.

pull it down to get the treat out of it. When he does, praise him and be sure that he gets the treat. Repeat this step several times, giving your rat the command "Pull it down."

- Now hold the cup even higher so that he won't be able to reach it and must pull on the string. You may need to show your rat how pulling on the string pulls the basket down. Make sure that he gets a treat every time he attempts this, even if he doesn't successfully pull on the string.
- Eventually your rat will understand that pulling down the string will pull down the cup containing the treat.

Once your rat understands that pulling on the string pulls the basket down, he may still need practice to learn the best technique for pulling down greater lengths of string.

## RING A BELL

It is easiest to teach ringing a bell after your rat learns the balloon pull-down. For this trick, you need to set up a bell that can be rung by being pulled on a string. Look in thrift shops for some sort of standing wire frame between 6 and 12 inches (15.2 and 30.5 cm) tall. I was able to find a wire-frame church that made a perfect prop, but you can use something like a simple wine rack. You can buy a small bell at a craft store.

- Cut a piece of string long enough to hang down from the top of the wire frame with an additional 5 inches (12.7 cm) that can rest on the ground. Tie one end to the bell. Then tie the end of the string with the bell attached to it to the top of the wire frame so that the bell hangs slightly below a top crosspiece of the wire frame.
- Dab a bit of food on the string at your rat's nose level, and encourage him to grab it with his teeth and/or hand. When he does so, reward him with a treat. If you prefer that your rat only pull the string with his hand, only reward him when he touches the string with his hand.
- Continue to encourage your rat to pull on the string, giving him a treat each time he tries. You may need to show him how to pull on the string with your fingers.
- Once it seems that your rat is getting the idea, don't reward each try but wait to see if he will do a bit better each time. Make him try two or three times before giving him the treat. At first he may not pull on the string hard enough to actually ring the bell. That's okay; continue to reward every second or third try.
- When your rat is routinely pulling on the string, only reward him if he pulls it hard enough to ring the bell.

Depending on your rat's ability, a prop trick can be simple or more detailed, such as pulling a wagon.

## RAISE A FLAG

In this trick, your rat will pull on a string that raises a small flag. Along with a flag, you will need some string and a wire frame. (See "Ring a Bell.") You can buy a small flag at most dollar stores, or you can make one by coloring a piece of paper and taping it to a pencil. This trick is taught in the same way as the bell trick described earlier, so after preparing your props, just follow the same steps.

- Tie a piece of string tightly around the flag's stick about one-third of the way up from the bottom.
- Tie the string to one of the upper crosspieces of the wire frame so that the flag hangs down from it.
- Tie another piece of string long enough to hang to the floor to the end of the flag. This is the string your rat will pull.

## UNFURL A BANNER

In this trick, your rat will pull a string that will unfurl a banner. You can make a banner with a small piece of fabric and a thin dowel. You will also need a wire frame (see "Ring a Bell") and some string. This trick is taught in the same way as the bell trick earlier, so after preparing your props, just follow the same steps.

- Cut a piece of fabric to the desired size. A 6-inch (15.2-cm) square works well. Write your message on the banner with felt pen, crayon, or paint.
- Cut the dowel into two pieces the length of the banner. Staple the pieces along the top and bottom of the banner.
- Tie the top dowel to the top crosspiece of the wire frame.
- Roll up the banner and secure it with a loose bow knot using a piece of string long enough to hang to the floor. This is the string your rat will pull to release the banner so that it will unfurl.

## PULL A WAGON

This trick requires a rat-sized wagon and harness. Look in a pet shop for a harness sold for small rodents, ferrets, or iguanas.

- First, place your rat on a table and put the harness on him. Let him get accustomed to the feel of it. If the harness fits him comfortably, it won't take long for him to get used to wearing it. When you think that the time is right, attach the harnss to the tongue of the wagon. (Attaching it to the tongue will keep the wagon from riding up on your rat's feet.)
- Next, lead your rat forward with a treat while giving the command "Pull." Initially, only have him pull it a few inches (several cm) before you reward him. Then gradually ask him to go farther each time.
- For the final step in the training sequence, stand at the other end of the table and hold the treat a few inches (several cm) from your rat. Have him come farther and farther to get the treat until he pulls the wagon all the way across the table.

## PUSH A BABY CARRIAGE/SHOPPING CART

The first step for this trick is to teach your rat to put his hands on the handle of the carriage or cart.

- Hold on to the cart to keep it from rolling or tipping over, and guide your rat with the treat so that he is in front of the handle.
- Then hold the treat over his head to get him to stand up. He will likely place a hand on the cart handle to steady himself, and when he does, give him the treat.
- Continue in this way until your rat will stand up with both hands on the handle.

- Now hold the treat farther in front of your rat's nose to encourage him to take a step. You can use the command "Let's shop" or "Let's stroll."
- Gently move the cart forward slightly. Give your rat the treat as soon as he takes a step. Continue in this way, asking your rat to take more and more steps before giving him the treat.

Until now, you have been holding the cart and controlling how far and fast it rolls forward. Now you will have to gradually lighten your hold on the cart to allow your rat to learn how much pressure to put on it to make it roll. If the cart is too light and tips over, you'll need to put an object in the cart to stabilize it. Once your rat learns the trick, you can put another rat in the cart!

**Push a carriage. The first step for this trick is to teach your rat to put his hands on the handles of the carriage. Later he will have to learn how to control how far and fast it rolls.**

## PUSH A SPOOL

This trick requires a spool (like those used for thread) and some wire. To prepare for training this trick, make a guide for the spool you are using as a prop by bending a piece of wire into the shape of an "L." Place the short leg of the wire into the hole of the spool. You should now have a handle with which you can roll the spool forward or backward. You will also need a clicker to mark correct behavior during training.

- Using the clicker, train your rat to touch the bottom of the spool with the top of his nose. This is the position his nose will have to be in to push the spool. Begin by putting the spool in front of your rat. Click and reward him for sniffing the spool.
- Wait for your rat to put his nose next to the spool again. When he does, click and reward him. Gradually wait for him to put his nose

## Perfectly Groomed

Before a performance, you want to prepare your rat to look his best. Rats groom themselves many times a day by licking their fur and combing it with their toenails, so it shouldn't be necessary to bathe a rat unless he has a health problem. However, not all rats clean their tail, and these appendages can sometimes look quite grubby. Keep your rat's tail clean by scrubbing it with soapy water and an old toothbrush. Not only will this help him make the best impression on his audience, but it will prevent infections that can occur if unshed scales accumulate there.

closer and closer to the bottom of the spool before you click and reward. Continue to do this until he finally places his nose at the right spot.

- Now use the wire guide to roll the spool away from him a fraction of an inch (a fraction of a centimeter). Again, click and reward your rat for touching the spool.
- Continue to shape your rat's behavior so that he will follow the spool for a distance, with his nose touching the spool as consistently as possible.
- Gradually reduce the pressure on the guide so that you aren't pushing the spool as much. Encourage your rat to push the spool with his nose instead. Use the command "Push." Click and reward him as needed.

At some point, you'll be able to take the wire guide away altogether. Then you will only click and reward when your rat actually pushes the spool instead of just touching it.

### BOWL

To prepare for this trick, make a ramp using a piece of wood about 12 to 18 inches (30.5 to 45.7 cm) long for the "bowling alley." You will also need a small ball and ten bowling pins. You can probably buy a tiny bowling set at dollar stores and novelty shops.

Before you begin training the complete trick, you'll have to teach your rat to push the ball. You teach this behavior in a similar way to pushing the spool. (See "Push a Spool.") This time, though, you only need your rat to give the ball one push, not to continue pushing it.

Once your rat knows how to push the ball, you can set up the rest of the equipment.

- Arrange the bowling pins in a triangle on the floor or on a table.
- Place one end of the ramp about 1 to 2 inches (2.5 to 5.1 cm) away from the point of the triangle.
- Place the other end of the ramp on a book about 3 inches (7.6 cm) thick. You will need to make a resting spot for the ball on the end of the ramp by putting two thumbtacks in the board just far enough apart so that the ball will rest against them. Make sure that your rat can push the ball over them.
- Place your rat on the book that the ramp is leaning against, and give him the command "Push" or "Bowl." Hopefully, the ball will roll down the ramp and knock down the pins.
- Reward your rat for pushing the ball down the ramp, and continue to practice until he does so consistently.

## PUSH A MARBLE UP A RAMP

This impressive trick takes more skill for a rat to learn than the previous two tricks because he will need to learn not only how to push the marble but how to control the direction in which the marble goes. The trick is much easier if

**Bowling.** Before you begin training the complete trick, you'll have to teach your rat to push a ball. Dabbing a bit of food on it will attract your rat and speed things up.

you make a groove down the center of the ramp in which to guide the marble.

It helps if your rat knows the spool trick first (see "Push a Spool") so that he will know how to push an object for a distance. After that, he will just need to practice learning how to control the marble.

- First, teach your rat to push the marble on a flat table, calling him to encourage him to push it to you. Each time he pushes the ball in the right direction (toward you), praise him and reward him with a treat.
- Next, teach your rat to push the marble on the ramp, which should be at least 4 inches (10.2 cm) wide, with the ramp lying flat at first. Each time he pushes the ball in the right direction (up the ramp), praise him and reward him with a treat.
- Gradually raise one end of the ramp about 1/4 inch (0.64 cm) at a time until there is a sufficient incline. Each time he pushes the ball up the ramp, praise him and reward him with a treat.

**If the prop you use produces a sound, the tone will provide audible feedback for your rat when he performs correctly.**

## PLAY THE PIANO, TYPE, OR DIAL A PHONE

All these tricks are taught in the same way; they are different only in the type of prop used. If the prop is one that will produce a tone when the keys or buttons are pushed, it will provide audible feedback for both your rat and you when he performs the trick correctly. The final goal is to only reward your rat when he pushes the buttons so that they produce a tone. However, the buttons may require more force than your rat can produce. If the prop does not produce a tone or your rat can't push the buttons hard enough, reward him for just touching the keys with his hand.

Some children's toy telephones produce a tone whenever the buttons are pushed. If you use a real phone for training, be careful that your rat doesn't end up dialing Japan! If you have a music program

# Photographing Your Rats in Action

Because rats tend to be very active, photographing them can be a challenge. Some rats run away whenever they see a camera. However, some actually like to pose. I have even discovered that some will take direction. For instance, I can ask one of my rats to lift his head, turn to the side, or look at the camera, and more times than not, he does what I ask! This is a thrilling experience.

The secret to getting good photographs of your rat is to get down to his level, move in close—you may need to use the macro setting on your camera—and be very patient. You'll often need to take a great many shots to get a few good pictures. This process is much easier (and less expensive) with digital photography than it used to be, but digital cameras can present an extra challenge. Most have a shutter delay that occurs between pressing the button and the moment it actually captures the picture. This delay lasts about a second or two, which may not seem very long, but it's long enough for your rat to change position or even move completely out of the frame. You'll have to anticipate your rat's movements and try to push the button before he reaches the pose you want.

Photographing your rat can be both frustrating and rewarding, but it's a great feeling when you finally get that perfect picture.

for your computer, you can set it up so that typing on the keyboard will also produce a tone. It is best to teach this trick with a clicker.

- Place your rat in front of the prop. Give the command "Play a song" (or "Type a letter" or "Make a call").
- At first, reward your rat for moving toward the prop, then for touching it with his hand.
- Once he is consistently touching the keys with his hands, you can train him to push the keys to produce a tone by gradually requiring that he push hard enough to make the tone. Give him a treat every time he produces a tone.
- Once your rat begins to understand the concept of the trick, you can require that he press more and more keys before getting his reward.

Initially, your rat may have a tendency to climb onto the prop to get closer to you and the treats. Gently put him back in place. If he wanders away from the prop, bring him back and show him the treat to keep his interest. You may want to give him a treat for returning to the prop, and occasionally give him one just for staying in the right place, even if he hasn't tried to press a key, just to keep his interest. This trick will take a lot of time and patience to teach.

# Chapter 9

# Games and Science Projects

**his** chapter contains activities you can do with your rat just for fun. Some of them can also be the basis for a science project. Teaching your rat these games and activities can provide him with mental stimulation and help increase his intelligence.

Aside from being interesting and enjoyable, though, you can learn a lot about rats by creating projects that explore how they tackle various tasks. Science projects in particular are designed to observe certain behaviors or to answer specific questions. For instance, a question you can explore using a Skinner box is: How many times will a rat press a lever to get one piece of food? With a T-maze, you can pursue a question such as: Can a rat tell the difference between spots and stripes? Or a question you can investigate using a racing lane is: Will a rat run faster to rock music or to country western music? So let the fun and games begin!

## THE SHELL GAME

Everyone has played the shell game at one time or another, but it is especially fun for an audience to watch your smart little pet attempt to beat this magic trick.

For the shell game, you need three small cups, but you will use just one cup to start. (The tiny, disposable plastic cups used at fast-food restaurants work well.) You will also need treats to place under the cups.

- First, teach your rat that he can find a treat under the cup. Do this by having him watch you place one there several times.
- Next, give him a command such as "Pick one" or "Which one?" You may need to draw his attention to the cup by tapping the table next to it or tapping the cup itself.
- Encourage your rat to sniff or push at the cup. As soon as he sniffs or touches the cup, lift it up so that he can get the treat.
- Once he knows that there is a treat under the cup, you can encourage him to knock the cup over to get the treat. Now you can bring in a second cup.
- Show your rat that you are putting the treat under one of the cups and give the command.
- Encourage your rat to go to one of the cups and sniff or touch it. Lift the cup to show your rat if there is a treat under the cup or not. If he picked the wrong cup, encourage

By trying to choose the cup under which you put a treat, your rat can learn to play the shell game.

him to go to the other cup and lift it so that he can get the treat.

- When your rat seems to understand that he needs to try to pick the right cup, you can start moving the cups around to mix them up. Of course, make sure that you replace the treat each time you restart the trick. (You may need to retrain your rat to stay to keep him away from the cups while you move them; see Chapter 7.)
- When you have the cups mixed up and are ready for your rat to make his choice, give him the command to pick one. If he picks the wrong cup, draw his attention to the right cup and give him the command again. You may need to lift the cup to show him the treat.
- Once he seems to understand that one of the cups will always have a treat under it, you can introduce a third cup. Repeat the preceding steps.

Until your rat seems to consistently understand the game, you should make sure that he always gets some treats for playing the game, regardless of whether he always picks the right cup.

## FAVORITE FOODS

This activity can be either a trick or a game, and it will really impress your friends by showing them how well your rat understands words.

- Pick two foods: your rat's favorite and another that he doesn't like as well.
- Work to teach your rat the names of these foods. You do this by repeating the word several times as you give him a piece of them.
- Every time you give your rat the food, say its name and repeat it while he eats it.
- After a few weeks, your rat should recognize these two words. You should be able to tell if he knows them by how he reacts to the different words; he should get excited when you say the name of his favorite food.

Now you can test your rat's food preferences and word knowledge with the help of another person. Each of you will have one of the two foods.

- Put your rat in between both of you.
- Each person should start repeating the name of the food she has. If your rat really understands the words, he should run to the person who has his favorite food. Of course, that person should immediately reward him with a piece of the food.
- Now try again, but this time switch foods. That way you'll know if your rat is really choosing his favorite food or his favorite person!

Once your rat knows how to play this game, you can teach him more words for foods, toys, or activities that will test his preferences and show off his intelligence.

# Science Fair Project Ideas

A simple science fair project could consist of seeing if your rat runs faster in the morning or at night. Another idea is to see whether using different foods for the reward changes a rat's racing time. Maybe your rat will run faster for avocado than for banana. For this project, you will need to run your rat several times using each food. You will probably want to use a different food each day and run at least ten trials for each food. Be sure to give your rat only a tiny bit of the food each time so that he won't fill up too fast.

## RACES

Racing can be a fun game for your rat or just a simple science fair project for you. One way to have a rat race is to teach him to run to you from any location, but you need another person to hold him in place at the start of the race.

You can make one or more racing lanes out of cardboard, plastic, or wood. (See Chapter 10 for construction plans.) You can also use one long 4-inch (10.2-cm) tube or several short tubes joined together to make a racing lane—you could even add curved ferret tubes for excitement. You won't be able to see your rat racing unless you use transparent tubes, but you should be able to hear his claws tapping their way down the tube.

- Before beginning to teach your rat to race, give him a chance to explore the racing lane. The best way to do this is to turn the lane on its side and let him enter and explore it on his own. With one of the sides acting as a roof, he will feel more secure in the new contraption. Put some food in one end of the lane and let your rat find it.
- Once he seems comfortable in the lane, you can take him out and turn the lane right-side up. Now hold your rat over the lane to see if he wants to get in. Don't force him into the lane because that might scare him.
- After he enters the lane, your rat may naturally proceed down the lane; if so, you just need to reward him with a treat when he reaches the opposite end.
- If he doesn't walk down the lane on his own, use a treat to lead him down it. Try not to give him the treat until he goes all the way to the finish line, but if he seems discouraged, go ahead and give him treats along the way.
- When he reaches the finish line, lift him out. Try not to let him go back the other way because you want him to learn to only run one way down the racing lane.
- Next, put your rat back in the lane and then move to the far end and encourage him to come by calling his name and saying "Come get the treat."
- Once he finds the treat, let him eat it and then lift him out of the lane.

The best way to get your rat to run fast is to use his favorite treat. After that, it's just a matter of practice until he runs right to the treat when you put him in the lane. But don't practice too much in one day. You don't want your rat to get tired or bored with either racing or his special treat.

It can be fun just to watch your rat race by himself. You could even time him if you have a stopwatch. But if you plan to race him against other rats, be sure that you practice two rats running together. They may be distracted by each other the first time. If the lanes are far enough apart, the distraction will be less. If you know someone else who has a rat, you might even pit your rats against each other, but be sure not to expose your pet to other rats unless they are healthy and have not been exposed to any strange rats for at least three weeks to reduce the risk of contracting infections.

## MAZES

Scientists often use mazes to study rat behavior because rats are burrowing animals who are good at finding their way through tunnels. However, it takes much longer for a rat to learn a complicated maze than most people expect. It can take many repetitions before a rat learns to run directly from the beginning of a maze to the food reward. It's best to start with a maze that isn't too complicated. Later, once the rat has learned the simple maze, you can advance to a more complex design. (For ideas on building mazes, see Chapter 10.)

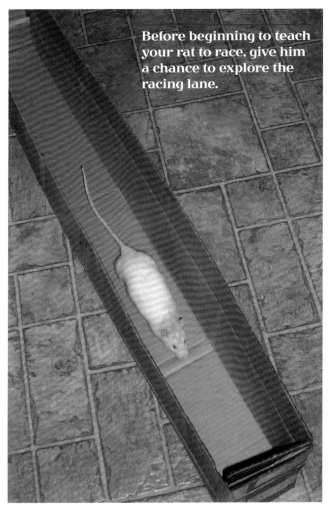

Before beginning to teach your rat to race, give him a chance to explore the racing lane.

### Acclimating to New Environments

When a rat is first placed in a maze, he is usually more interested in exploring this new environment than eating any treats. Rats are very curious creatures, and exploration is one of their primary joys in life. So to begin with, don't bother to put any food in the maze. Instead, just let your rat wander through the hallways. Even though he isn't trying to reach a goal, he will still be learning the maze. The next time you put him in the maze, you can put a treat at one end and wait for him to find it.

Here's how to train your rat to use a simple maze:

- Pick a location in the maze for the starting area of the trial run.
- Next, choose the spot in the maze you want your rat to find. Put a treat in that location; this will be the end point of the trial run.
- Place your rat in the starting area and let him explore the maze. If you want to

# Rats and Maze IQ

Scientific studies have shown that male and female rats learn mazes differently, just as men and women tend to learn their way to the corner store differently. Males are more likely to memorize the path of the maze—how many right turns and how many left turns. Females are more likely to use landmarks instead, both in the maze and in the room, such as marks on the wall or the location of ceiling lights. It just goes to show that there is more than one kind of "intelligence." Do mazes test the intelligence of rats? Well, we only know for sure that it tests how well they can remember mazes!

time the trial, start recording the time as soon as you put him in the starting area.

- When your rat finds the treat, stop recording the time. Let him eat the treat, then remove him from the maze. Do not let him wander in the maze after eating the treat.
- Repeat this procedure for each trial run.

### Discrimination T-Maze

The T-maze is a very simple maze that really isn't much of a maze at all. Instead, it is a tool used in behavior research to study discrimination, or the ability of animals to remember and make choices. This maze is shaped—as its name suggests—like the letter "T." The rat is placed at the bottom of the T, and when he gets to the arms of the T, he must choose whether to go right or left. The rat will only get a reward if he makes the right choice.

The researcher usually gives the rat a visual clue by using a pattern on the inside walls of the arms (the top of the T). The pattern could be on all the walls of the arm or only the far wall. For instance, a rat might be trained to pick the white side, while another might be trained to pick the black side. Or the rat might be trained to choose a striped pattern instead of a spotted pattern. Rats are mostly colorblind, so it is very difficult to test them on different colors.

The behavioral study gets interesting when the rat is then asked to choose the opposite selection. How long does it take him to learn to choose the other pattern? In general, the more intelligent the subject is, the quicker he will learn to reverse his choice.

To use a T-maze for discrimination studies, it must be constructed so that the arms of the maze can be quickly and easily detached and switched. If the same pattern always appears in the left-hand arm, the rat may not be learning to choose the pattern on the walls but simply learning to always turn to the left. During the training, the arms must be switched frequently so that the rat must sometimes turn right and sometimes turn left to make the correct choice. (For instructions for making a T-maze, see Chapter 10.)

Before beginning the discrimination trials, let your rat explore the maze to get used to it, then remove him from the maze and place him in a holding cage equipped with a water bottle.

- Put a small food reward at the end of the arm of the maze containing the pattern that you want to reward.
- Place your rat at the bottom of the T-maze, and let him explore it. If he

It can take many repetitions before a rat learns to run directly from the beginning of a maze to the food reward. It's best to start with a maze that isn't too complicated.

chooses to enter the correct arm, let him eat the treat and then take him out and put him back into the holding cage. If he goes into the incorrect arm of the maze (the one containing the wrong pattern), take him out as soon as he reaches the end of it. This is one trial. Be sure to record your rat's choice if you are running a science project.

- You need to randomly select the pattern that will be on either side of the maze for each trial. A good way to do this is to flip a coin. If it comes up heads, the arrangement stays the same; if it comes up tails, you switch the patterns.
- Repeat this procedure for each successive trial. You will probably want to run between 15 and 25 trials at a time.

If you want to study more than two different patterns, you might want to make spare maze arms. Or you might design the arms so that the patterns can be easily changed; for example, you might want to take out the "wallpaper" of one pattern and put up another.

The T-maze can also be used to test your rat's food preferences. In this case, your rat gets a treat in both arms of the maze—a different food in each. You can always put the same food on the same side, or if you pair a food with a pattern, the rat will eventually associate the two and know what food is waiting for him at the end of the maze by looking at the pattern on the wall. That way, the rat can learn to choose his favorite food.

For instance, let's say you put a tiny piece of avocado—a common rat favorite—in one arm of the maze and pair it with white walls. In the other arm you put a piece of broccoli or carrot, foods that many rats like but usually not as much as avocado. The second food can be paired with black walls. As in other tests, you need to randomly switch the arms of the maze for each trial.

There are several things you can study with this protocol. You can see how long it takes a rat to learn the association between the food and pattern—that is, how long it takes before the rat consistently chooses the same food each trial. You can also see if the rat's fondness for the food correlates with the learning time. For instance, does your rat learn the association faster with a favorite food compared to a less favorite food?

Once your rat learns the food/pattern associations, you can do a reverse discrimination choice test to see how long it takes for him to learn that the avocado is now paired with the black walls. Again, does the rat's fondness for a food shorten the learning time, or perhaps does it lengthen it because the rat doesn't want to give up a favorite association? There are many possible protocols, and all are fascinating experiments.

## Radial Maze

Another type of maze that scientists sometimes use is a radial maze. This

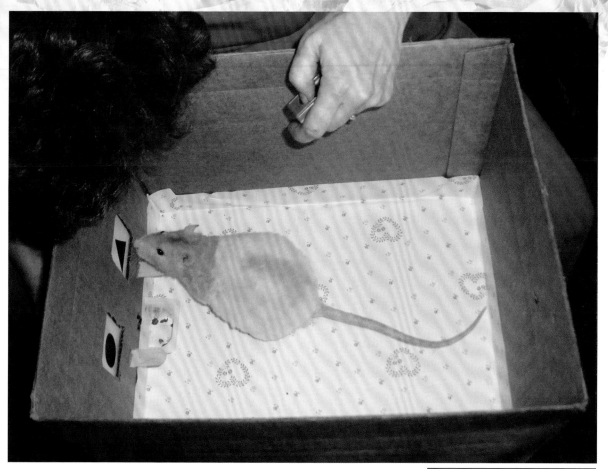

design is like a sun with a center hub, with the arms of the maze radiating outward like sun rays. The rat is placed in the center and is allowed to choose from all the different arms of the maze. This lets scientists study how well rats can remember different locations. For instance, they might put rewards in only every other arm and see how long it takes the rat to learn that every other arm is empty.

Scientists have also used radial mazes to see how well a rat can remember which arms they have already visited. They put food at the end of each arm and then record which arms the rat visits. Test results have shown that most rats are very good at remembering which arms they have already visited to eat the food so that they won't waste their time visiting them again.

**The Skinner box is a common tool used to study learning skills in animals. The box restricts the animal's movements to help keep his attention on the training task.**

# Science Projects With the Skinner Box

To use a Skinner box for a science project, you need to pick a question that can be answered by teaching your rat to press the lever in response to a stimulus. For example: Can a rat learn the difference between a circle and a square? In this case, you will need two levers in the box and a window over each lever. In one window you will put a card with a circle, and in the other you will put a card with a square. You must be able to switch the cards between the two windows so that sometimes the rat must press the right lever and sometimes the left lever. Decide if you want your rat to pick the circle or the square, and only reward him for pressing the correct lever. Let's say that you decide on the circle. If your rat learns to always press the lever below the circle, you will know that he can tell the difference between a circle and a square.

Here are some ideas for other science projects:

- Can a rat tell the difference between a small circle and a large circle? How similar must the sizes of the two circles be before the rat can no longer tell the difference between them?
- Can a rat learn to keep track of time? If he must wait one minute between rewards, will he continue to press the lever in between or will he take a one-minute break?
- Can a rat tell the difference between a rap song and a rock song? Can he learn to press the left lever while a rap song is playing and the right lever when a rock song plays? Can he generalize this choice so that he can make the correct choice between any rap or rock music?

You can also set up a science project to study the differences among several rats. For example, do some rats learn a task much faster or slower than other rats?

# THE SKINNER BOX

An apparatus called an operant conditioning chamber is more commonly called a Skinner box, named after the scientist B.F. Skinner, who invented it. The Skinner box has become a common tool used to study learning skills in different animals. The box restricts the animal's movements to help keep his attention on the training task, and it also limits the number of behaviors in which the animal can engage.

The most common type of Skinner box used for rats has one or more levers that the rat can push down. The box must also provide a way to reward the rat, usually a food hopper where the rat can go to get a tasty food pellet. In the laboratory, a Skinner box also usually includes lights that are used as signals to the rat and sometimes windows where various symbols or colors can be displayed. (For instructions on how to build a simple Skinner box, see Chapter 10.)

The training method used with a Skinner box is shaping, the same method used in clicker training. (See Chapter 3.) The sound of the food reward being dropped into the food hopper can act as the bridge to the behavior you want him to perform. If the treat dropping into the hopper doesn't make a sound, you'll need to use a clicker or another sound for the secondary reinforcer.

- When you put your rat into the Skinner box for the first time, give him a chance to explore it thoroughly.
- After he seems comfortable in the box (he will probably start to groom himself), drop a treat in the food hopper. If he doesn't notice, make a gentle scratching noise near the food hopper to attract his attention and lead him to the hopper.
- Once he finds the food and eats it, put another treat in the hopper. Do this about five times so that he knows for sure where he can find the treats.
- To teach your rat to press the lever, wait until he moves his head toward the lever, no matter how slightly. Immediately give him a reward.
- Again, wait for him to make any movement toward the lever and then put a treat in the hopper. He should start moving slightly back and forth between the hopper and lever.
- Next, wait before giving him a treat to see if he will move closer to the lever. When he does, reward him. If he doesn't, you must wait until he makes a small movement toward the lever again.
- Gradually wait to reward him until he is moving closer and closer to the lever.
- Once he is close enough to the lever to touch it, wait until he moves one of his hands toward the lever and reward him.

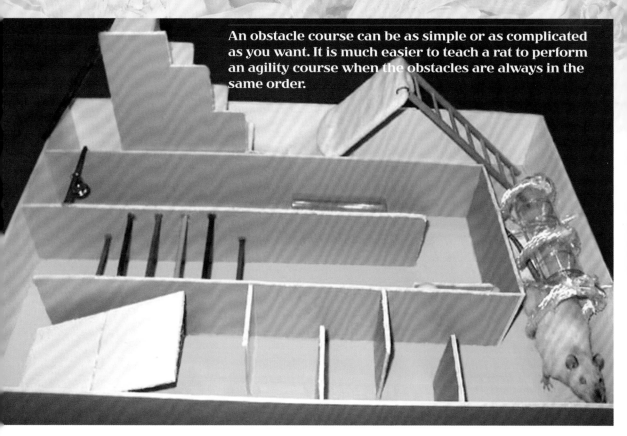

An obstacle course can be as simple or as complicated as you want. It is much easier to teach a rat to perform an agility course when the obstacles are always in the same order.

- Then wait until he moves his hand closer to the lever. In this way, shape his behavior until he is touching the lever with his entire hand.
- Next, wait until he puts some pressure on the lever with his hand before rewarding him.
- Gradually shape his behavior until he is pushing all the way down on the lever. By the time your rat has pressed the lever five times, he will know that that's what you want him to do. That's it—you have trained your rat to press the lever!

You can train your rat to do other behaviors in the Skinner box. For instance, you can teach him to turn in a circle and then press the lever, or you can have him just turn in a circle. You could also teach him to put his head in one corner or to stand on his hind legs and then turn in a circle. Or you could teach him to jump up and touch a spot on the wall. The only limits to what you can teach your rat in a Skinner box depend on his physical capabilities, as well as your time and patience.

# OBSTACLE COURSES AND AGILITY TRAINING

A fun activity for both you and your pet rat is to set up a series of obstacles and then teach him to negotiate them. There are also lots of variations on this activity that will provide hours of fun and stimulation for your small companion.

## Obstacle Courses

An obstacle course can be as simple or as complicated as you want. Rats are very athletic and can perform well on a variety of different hurdles and barriers. You can set up the obstacles and always keep them in the same order, or you can move them around. Obstacles used for this activity can be similar to those used in a competition held for dogs called an agility trial. In fact, some rat clubs even hold agility competitions for rats.

## Training a Rat on the Obstacles

It is much easier to teach a rat to perform an agility course when the obstacles are always in the same order. In this case, you can use the chaining technique (see Chapter 3): You must teach your rat to do the last obstacle first, then the second to last, etc. However, the order in which you teach the obstacles may depend on which obstacles are easier to teach. For example, on an agility course used in Finland, the bridge, which is one of the easiest obstacles to teach, is first, while the teeter-totter, a more difficult obstacle to teach, is last. In this case, you probably want to teach the bridge first because it's the easiest obstacle for a rat to learn. Once a rat learns the first obstacle, it will be easier to teach the harder ones. At this point, you can switch to chaining to teach the remaining obstacles in reverse order, from last to first. After you teach each new obstacle, have your rat perform that obstacle and then continue to complete the rest of the course from that point on. This will help your rat develop the habit of running the whole course without stopping.

Because using food is not allowed during agility competition, some people like to train their rats to do agility without using food. They do this by using the rat's natural curiosity and praising him for learning each obstacle. In dog agility, most people use food to train their dogs, and once the dog understands the obstacles, they begin to replace the food with praise to prepare him for competition. But most will use food during training to maintain the dog's motivation. I recommend using food to teach rats to do agility.

To teach each obstacle, you can use the leading method (using food to lead your rat in the correct path), or the targeting method (using a target, such as the eraser end of a pencil) to lead your rat over the obstacles. Both methods are similar. I suggest using the leading method until your rats are more experienced.

**The bridge. When teaching your rat to perform the bridge, make sure that he doesn't jump off too soon.**

This obstacle course will include a bridge, weave poles, jumping poles, a hoop, an A-frame, a teeter-totter, and a tube. How impressive! (For information on building obstacles, see Chapter 10.)

### Bridge

To teach your rat to run the bridge using the leading method, do the following:

- Using a food treat, lead your rat up onto the bridge. As soon as he is on the bridge, reward him with the treat.
- Next, again using a food treat, lead your rat along the bridge and then down off the other end. The main problem will be keeping him from jumping off the bridge prematurely. To prevent this behavior, never give the treat if your rat jumps off the bridge before finishing the task (reaching the end of the bridge and stepping off of it). Make him go back to the beginning and complete the task properly before giving him the reward. (However, it is okay to give him a treat if he stops on the bridge while he is learning to complete the exercise.)

You will teach the other obstacles in the same way.

## Weave Poles

For the weave poles, lead your rat though the poles with the food treat. You may need to give him a treat part of the way through the pole course during the training process, but try to make sure that he goes all the way through the course each time. You do not want him to get into the habit of only going part of the way through and then leaving it. This obstacle takes a lot of patience and practice to teach.

## Hoop

Teaching the hoop jump is fairly easy. Just make sure that once your rat understands how to go through the hoop you make him climb completely through before giving him a reward. Teaching a pole jump is also quite easy. Just make sure that your rat makes it all the way over the jump with all four feet on the floor before giving him the treat.

## A-Frame

Teaching the A-frame for competition is harder then you might think because the bottom third of each side of the A-frame is the "contact zone." To properly negotiate this obstacle during competition, the rat must place at

# Rat Agility Competition

Rat agility competitions have become quite popular. Many rat shows in England, Finland, and Sweden include a chance for rats to compete in this category. In some of the clubs, rat agility is like dog agility competition in that the obstacles can be arranged in a different order for each individual trial. In other clubs, the obstacles are always kept in the same order.

If you are interested in running agility trials with your pets, you can learn more about training and competition requirements by researching rat clubs and rat agility on the web. You can also see wonderful examples of rats doing tricks and running obstacle and agility courses on various websites...as they say a picture is worth a thousand words. Here are a few that offer informative photos as well as useful information:

- www.neratsociety.co.uk/images/Agility/agility_training.htm
- theagilerat.com
- ratz.co.uk/agility

When teaching the teeter-totter, you must hold the board and keep it under control so that your rat doesn't get scared.

least one foot in each contact zone rather than just jumping past them. When making the A-frame, the contact zones should be marked in some way. Both rats and dogs have a tendency to jump over the contact zones. To prevent this, use the food to lead your rat slowly up one side of the A-frame and then slowly down the other side, making sure that he doesn't jump off part of the way.

### Teeter-Totter

When teaching the teeter-totter, you must hold the board and keep it under control so that your rat doesn't get scared. If the board tips too quickly, the rat will feel like he is falling and he won't be too willing to get on it again. Start gradually tipping the board as the rat approaches the center, before his weight makes it move, so that he will get used to the motion. As your rat becomes more accustomed to the movement, you can let his own body weight tip the board, but you should still keep it under control. Encourage him to move past the center of the board slowly so that the board won't tip too quickly. Eventually, your rat should be able to do the teeter-totter by himself.

### Tube

When it comes to teaching the tube, especially the long tube, the problem isn't getting the rat to go into the tube but getting him to come out! Be patient at first and give him a little time inside. As the training progresses, use more coaxing to try to get him to come out—use treats if you must! You may even have to put your hand into the tube and push him out from behind. And remember, no matter how hard it was to get him to come out, be sure to give him a treat and lots of praise and petting when he finally does. For variety, you can use a curved or wiggly tube instead of or in addition to the straight tube.

## MORE IDEAS

Most of the tricks in Chapters 7, 8, and 9 use props that can be incorporated into an obstacle course. For people who are handy and can figure out how to make things, here are a few other ideas for additional obstacles you can create:

- ladder
- staircase
- spiral ramp

I have also seen more complicated ideas for obstacles you can create. Imagine how much excitement these would add to your obstacle course:

- Drawbridge: The bridge starts in a vertical position, and the rat must use his weight to lower the bridge.
- Pedal car: The rat gets in the car and pedals it to make it move.
- Elevator: The elevator will be designed to go down when the rat gets into it. (The elevator will require a mechanical device [counterweights] to make it go up and down.)
- Ladder pull-up: The rat pulls a string that raises a ladder to the next level.
- Sliding hanging basket: The rat gets into a basket that slides down a wire.
- Swinging basket: The rat pulls the basket to him with a string, gets in the basket, and swings over to a shelf.

## MORE THAN FUN AND GAMES

Before I became "The Rat Lady" in 1995, I was known as Debbie "The Dog Lady" because I taught dog obedience classes and was very much involved in training my dogs to compete in obedience and agility trials, as well as to do tricks. But once I made the switch to rats, I found that they satisfied all my needs for companionship, interaction, and affection. I don't miss having dogs and may never own a dog again.

Every year I make several appearances with my rats at different events to show people how much fun it can be to teach their rats to do tricks. The rats who perform with me show every sign of enjoying the attention and the chance to show off. All pets thrive on attention, and when you teach rats to do tricks, they love the opportunity to spend extra time with you. Teaching rats tricks strengthens the bond between you, offers them necessary mental stimulation and physical exercise, and is lots of fun for all involved. I wish you and your rat lots of fun and tricks!

# Chapter 10
# Project Plans for Tricks

A ll the objects for the project plans in this section can be made from wood, cardboard, or a material called Coroplast. Each of these materials has advantages and drawbacks.

Objects made from wood are more durable but also heavier and harder to build. Wood should be painted or protected with some type of finish to protect it from urine.

Coroplast is the name of a special corrugated plastic signboard available at sign shops. Lightweight, waterproof, and fairly durable, it comes in 4-foot by 8-foot (10.2-cm by 20.3-cm) sheets in many colors. When buying it at a sign shop, tell them what you want it for and they might give you a good price and even help you cut it. You may want to bring heavy scissors to cut it yourself at the shop so that you can get it into your car just in case.

Cardboard is lightweight, easy to work with, and readily available. A good place to look for large or long cardboard boxes is a moving company. Cardboard and wood can be protected with an adhesive contact paper covering, which you can buy at most variety and hardware stores.

Most of the instructions here are for cardboard, but they can be easily modified for Coroplast or wood.

## RACING LANES

You can make racing lanes any size you like, but I suggest that you make them 5 to 6 inches (12.7 to 15.2 cm) wide, 8 inches (20.3 cm) high, and at least 5 feet ( 1.5 m) long. If you're going to make more than one racing lane, you can make each one slightly larger than the previous one so that they can be stacked inside each other for storage.

Because many rats seem to find tape very interesting to chew on or eat, I suggest

## ILLUSTRATION 1: RACING LANE

5-6 inches
(12.7-
15.2 cm)

8 inches

8 inches
(20.3 cm)

that you try to make the racing lanes without using tape on the inside.

**Step 1:** The lane will be strongest if you can make it all in one piece. First determine how long you want the lane to be. If you need to join two pieces of cardboard or Coroplast together to make a longer piece, overlap the pieces at least 2 inches (5.1 cm) for strength, and only tape them together on the side that will be on the outside of the lane.

**Step 2:** Cut out the lane as shown in illustration 1.

**Step 3:** Fold along the dotted lines. To ensure that the cardboard folds straight, lay it along the straight edge of a table and press down on each side close to the fold line.

**Step 4:** Tape the lane together using tape only on the outside.

## MAZE

A large cardboard box at least 8 inches (20.3 cm) high makes a great base for a maze. If necessary, you can cut a taller box shorter. You will also need several pieces of cardboard about 8 inches (20.3 cm) tall for the inside walls of the maze. You can use a few small boxes to make these. Just cut off the flaps and cut along the seam of the box so that you can open the box flat. You can leave the four walls of the small box attached to each other for support, or cut them apart. Also, buy a box of 16d 3½-inch (8.9-cm or equivalent) box nails. These will be the supports for the maze walls.

**Step 1:** Draw out the plan for your maze. Remember that it's is best to start with a simple maze. You can always add to it later as your rat learns how to run it.

**Step 2:** Decide on the measurements for your maze, and make a list of all the walls and their sizes. For instance, for the plan shown in illustration 2, you need one wall 20 inches (50.8 cm) long, one wall 15 inches (38.1 cm) long, and one wall 10 inches (25.4 cm) long. The wall that includes two corners will be strongest if it can be made in one piece. To do this you'll need a piece 35 inches (88.9 cm) long folded twice. Or you can use one piece 10 inches (25.4 cm) long and one piece 25 inches (63.5 cm) long folded once, or use one piece 15 inches (38.1 cm) long and one 20 inches (50.8 cm) long folded once.

**Step 3:** Cut out the walls.

**Step 4:** If the box has flaps on the top, cut them off. Draw lines on the floor of the maze box to show where the walls go. Poke holes for the nails along each line 3 to 4 inches (7.6 to 10.2 cm) apart. Insert the nails up through the holes from the bottom of the box. Tape the nails in place. Carefully align each wall with its nails. Now push the wall down onto the nails so that the nails go up into the corrugated spaces within the cardboard. You have a maze!

## T-MAZE

The T-maze is constructed much like the racing lane. There are three pieces: the entrance corridor and two arms. The arms are separate so that they can be switched from side to side. Your rat will enter each of the arms through a hole cut in the wall of the entrance corridor. When you fold the end of the entrance corridor where the arms will attach, you need to cut off 2 inches (5.1 cm) of the flaps, as shown in illustration 3. Attach the arms to the entrance corridor lightly with a few pieces of tape.

## ILLUSTRATION 2: MAZE

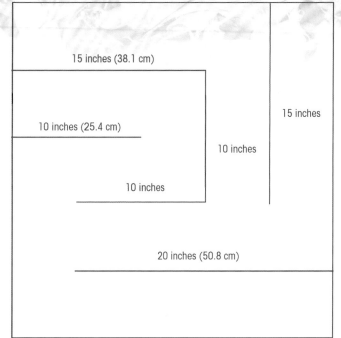

15 inches (38.1 cm)

10 inches (25.4 cm)

15 inches

10 inches

10 inches

20 inches (50.8 cm)

## ILLUSTRATION 3: (A) T-MAZE (B) ENTRANCE ARM

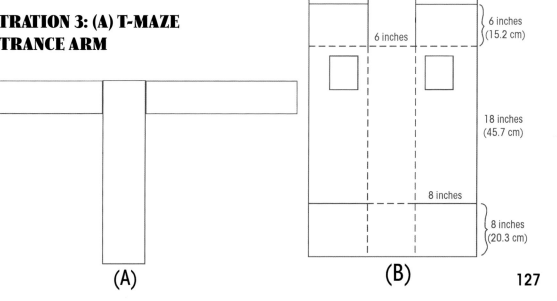

6 inches

6 inches (15.2 cm)

18 inches (45.7 cm)

8 inches

8 inches (20.3 cm)

(A)

(B)

127

## ILLUSTRATION 4: (A) SKINNER BOX (B)LEVERS

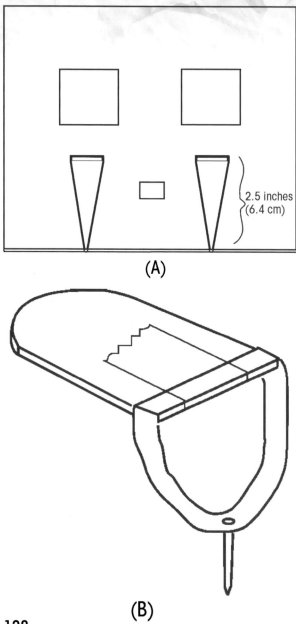

(A)

(B)

2.5 inches (6.4 cm)

## SKINNER BOX

You'll need a box about 14 inches (35.6 cm) square and at least 8 inches (20.3 cm) tall. It's a good idea to line the box with adhesive contact paper so that any messes can be wiped up easily.

**Step 1:** A wooden tongue depressor works well for a lever. (Ask your doctor or veterinarian for one.) You can also use a craft stick, which you can buy at a craft store. Cut each lever 2 inches (5.1 cm) long from the rounded end. Tape a wide rubber band to the cut end of the stick as shown in illustration 4. Poke a 1-inch (2.5-cm) nail through the other end of the rubber band.

**Step 2:** You need to cut a slot in the wall of the box for each lever you want to make, plus a small hole for the treat delivery. For just one lever, make the slot on one side of one wall and the treat window next to it. For two levers, make the slots evenly spaced on one wall, with the treat hole in the middle. Put the slots 2½ inches (6.4 cm) high. Cut each slot carefully—just the width of the stick—so that each stick fits snugly in its slot.

**Step 3:** Insert each lever through its slot so that the end with the rubber band is on the outside with the rubber band hanging down. Attach the nail to the box by poking it between the layers of cardboard on the bottom of the box. There should be slight tension on the rubber band when the lever is in the up position.

**Step 4:** Cut a hole about 1/2 inch (1.27 cm) square for the treat hole. Underneath the hole, attach a little container to catch the treat. It works well to use a plastic baby food container (a short one). Cut the container in half, and tape or glue it under the treat hole.

**Step 5:** If you want to train your rat to respond to different visual shapes, cut out one or more windows so that you can change the shapes from outside the box. You can tape a card showing a shape to the outside of the box so that it shows through the window.

If you want, you can make one window for each lever. Make each window 2 inches (5.1 cm) square and 3½ inches (8.9 cm) above the floor of the box. If you'd like, cut only the sides and bottom of a window, leaving the square of cardboard attached at the top. You can then close the window.

## AGILITY OBSTACLES

You can find pictures of rat agility obstacles on the Internet if you search for "rat agility."

### A-Frame

The easiest way to make an A-frame is to use a cardboard box about 6 to 8 inches (15.2 to 20.3 cm) tall, 11 inches (28 cm) wide and 17 inches (43 cm) long. If you can't find a box this size, ask at a print shop for one of the boxes that bulk paper comes in (some are more sturdy than others) and cut it shorter.

**ILLUSTRATION 5: A-FRAME**

**Step 1:** If using a bulk paper box, choose one of the corners and cut from the top of the box to the bottom. Then cut the bottom off the box. If the box has flaps, cut them all off as well. Cut the box apart and lay it flat. See illustration 5.

**Step 2:** Fold up the box to form a triangle as shown. Cut off the extra cardboard at the end. Voilà! You have an A-frame. Tape it together.

**Step 3:** If the ramps need more support, you can cut additional pieces of cardboard to brace the inside of the A-frame. Or you can stuff crumpled paper inside to provide support.

**Step 4:** Now you need to add a nonslip surface to the ramps to prevent your rat from slipping. A good choice is a product sold for the bottom of a bathtub. Or you can make and attach rungs made of cardboard or wood to the ramps to provide traction. I usually glue on craft sticks.

**Step 5:** For competition, the bottom third of each ramp should be marked—or even painted a different color—as the "contact zone." To properly negotiate this obstacle during competition, the rat must place at least one foot in each contact zone rather than jumping past them. A rat who jumps over a contact zone will lose points.

### Weave Poles

This version is slightly different from the weave poles used in dog agility; the poles are offset rather than in a straight line to make it easier for the rat. If building the weave poles from wood, use 1-inch (2.5-cm) wooden dowels for the poles.

**Step 1:** Cut a piece of cardboard 6 inches (15.2 cm) wide and 16 inches (40.6 cm) long. This will be the base platform for the weave poles.

**Step 2:** Decide where you want to put the poles. The closer they are to a straight line, the more difficult it will be for your rat to weave between them. A wider corridor is easier for your rat to go through. Mark the spots for the poles on the cardboard.

**Step 3:** With a sharp pair of scissors, carefully poke a hole through the cardboard at each spot. At each spot cut an X just over 1/2 inch (1.27 cm) across.

**Step 4:** For poles, you can buy disposable 12 cc syringes at a pharmacy. You will need five. Insert one plunger into each X cut into the platform base from the bottom up. Tape the plungers in place underneath. These will serve as supports for the poles.

**Step 5:** Take five empty cardboard toilet paper tubes, and cut each one lengthwise. Roll a tube tightly around each one of the plunger supports and tape in place.

### Teeter-Totter

**Step 1:** Cut a piece of Masonite board, thin plywood, or other strong thin board 4 inches (10.2 cm) wide and 14 inches (35.6 cm) long. Smooth off any rough edges with sandpaper or a file. You can also tape four wooden paint stirrers or wooden rulers together side by side with packing tape to make a board.

**Step 2:** Tape a cardboard toilet paper tube to the center underside of the board. Then take about seven other toilet paper tubes, cut them lengthwise, roll them up, and place them inside the tube taped to the bottom of the teeter-totter. This will provide more support.

### Rat-Walk or Bridge

**Step 1:** The easiest way to make the bridge is with three wooden or aluminum rulers. taped to the tops of two 6-inch (15.2-cm) flowerpots turned upside down. (I get my flowerpots from a thrift store.)

## Hoop Jump

**Step 1:** The easiest way to make a hoop jump is with the empty cardboard center from a roll of masking or packing tape. You can also cut a hoop from an oatmeal box, or just cut a strip of fiberboard, bend it into a hoop, and tape it together.

**Step 2:** Tape the cardboard hoop vertically onto a small sturdy bowl turned upside down.

## Fence Jump

**Step 1:** Using a copy machine, enlarge the patterns shown in illustration 6 by 200 percent. Cut out the patterns and trace them onto a piece of heavy cardboard.

**Step 2:** Cut out the cardboard patterns.

**Step 3:** Fold the cardboard along the dotted lines. To make sure that the cardboard folds properly, lay it along the straight edge of a table and press down on each side close to the fold line. Tape or glue the two sides of the fence together.

**Step 4:** Tape or glue the cardboard triangles to the fence supports.

## Basketball Hoop

You can sometimes find a rat-sized basketball hoop for sale in toy stores, thrift shops, or dollar stores. Because these hoops cannot be lowered and raised for training, you will need to have a platform for the rat to stand on to reach the basket, which can be gradually lowered. (See how the Center for Science and Industry [COSI] its their rats to play basketball in Chapter 7.)

## Making an Adjustable Basketball Hoop
### Materials Needed

- 3/16 inch (0.48 cm) steel rod, 10 inches (25.4 cm) long
- 1/2-inch-thick (1.27-cm-thick) wood, 5½ (14 cm) inches square
- 14 gauge fence wire, 14 inches (35.6 cm) long
- thin wire or twist ties
- one window security lock
- cardboard, foam board, or Coroplast, 4½ (11.4 cm) inches by 3½ (8.9 cm) inches
- heavy cotton string (optional)
- paint (optional)

## ILLUSTRATION 6: FENCE JUMP

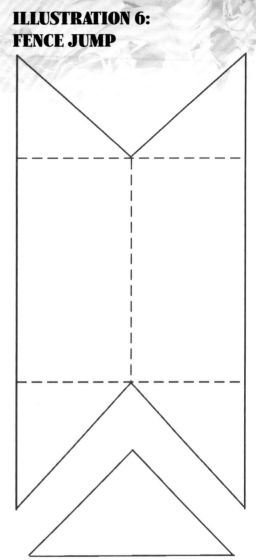

**Tools Needed**
- scissors
- needle-nose pliers
- saw
- drill and 3/16 inch (0.48 cm) bit

**Step 1:** The base: Cut the 1/2-inch-thick (1.27-cm-thick) wood to size with the saw. Drill a 3/16-inch (0.48-cm) hole in the center. Insert the rod.

**Step 2:** The net: You can probably find a small, cheap basketball hoop for sale at a dollar store or grocery store that has a net you can take off and use. If not, you can make one out of the cotton string. Cut five pieces of string, each 14 inches (35.6 cm) long. Lay them out as shown in illustration 7(a) and knot them together. Tie the knots 1/2 inch (1.27 cm) apart. Form the net into a circle by knotting the two ends together. Cut off the surplus string under the last knots.

**Step 3:** The hoop: Bend the fence wire as shown in illustration 7(b) so that it makes a circle 3 inches (7.6 cm) across. Thread the wire through the upper loops of the net.

**Step 4:** The backstop: Cut out the cardboard backstop and paint it if desired. Poke two pairs of holes in the cardboard 1/2 inch (1.27 cm) apart as shown in illustration 7(c) and 7(d). Stick the ends of the hoop wires through the bottom holes of the backstop, then bend them across the back of the backstop so that the steel rod can be inserted between the cardboard and the wires. Adjust the bend in the wire so that the hoop is level. Lower the backstop over the steel rod. Put the thin wire or twist tie through the upper holes and around the rod. The wires should be snug but not tight.

**Step 5:** The window security lock is the support for the backboard so that you can easily move the hoop up and down for training. Put the groove of the lock over the pole so that when you tighten the screw, it will hold the pole firmly. The flat part of the lock should face away from the backboard. Move the lock up the pole, and gently pull the bottom of the backboard out so that you can slide the lock up behind the backboard until it fits snugly against the wires. To change the height of the basket, just loosen the screw slightly and gently move the whole assembly up or down.

# ILLUSTRATION 7: (A) HOOP NET (B) FENCE-WIRE HOOP (C) BACKSTOP (D) COMPLETE BASKETBALL PROP

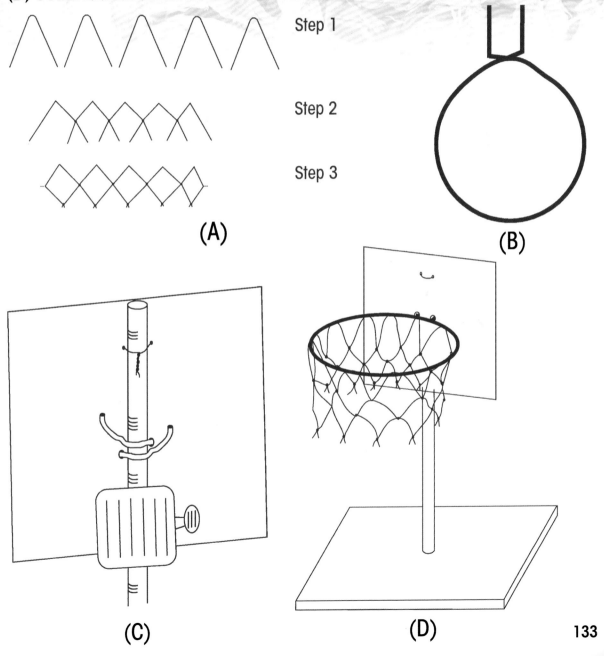

Step 1

Step 2

Step 3

(A)

(B)

(C)

(D)

# Appendix

## INTELLIGENCE TEST

This is a simple questionnaire that will help you judge how smart your rat is. It is based on a questionnaire in another book, *Mysteries of Animal Intelligence: True Stories of Animals With Amazing Abilities*[1], by Sherry Hansen Steiger and Brad Steiger, but I have modified it for rats. Keep in mind that personality traits can mask intelligence. A rat who is very shy, nervous, active, or independent may score low on the test even with a high IQ.

For each question, pick the option that best describes your rat. Then add up the points.

### 1. Your rat:
(a) always listens when you talk to him and seems to understand a lot of what you say—5 points
(b) sometimes listens when you talk to him and seems to understand some of what you say—4 points
(c) sometimes seems to listen to what you say to him but doesn't seem to understand—2 points
(d) seldom seems to listen when you talk—1 point

### 2. Your rat:
(a) always comes when you call—5 points
(b) sometimes comes when you call—3 points
(c) occasionally comes when you call—1 point

### 3. Your rat:
(a) is always curious about new things, places, and people—5 points
(b) is sometimes curious about new things, places, and people—3 points
(c) is occasionally curious about new things, places, and people—1 point
(d) does not seem curious about new things, places, and people—0 points

### 4. If your rat is eating a large piece of food and you offer him a piece of food he likes better, he:
(a) immediately drops the food he is eating to take the new food—5 points
(b) tries to take the new food but can't with food already

in his mouth, so he then drops the food to take the new food—4 points
(c) tries to take the new food but can't with food already in his mouth, but he persists in trying—2 points
(d) tries to take the new food but can't with food already in his mouth, so he gives up and continues eating the original food—1 point

### 5. Let your rat watch you hide a treat under a cup or in your hand. Your rat:
(a) can immediately find the treat—5 points
(b) looks for the treat but has trouble remembering where you put it—3 points
(c) forgets all about the treat when you hide it—0 points

### 6. Your rat learns tricks in:
(a) one to three lessons—5 points
(b) four to six lessons—4 points
(c) seven to nine lessons—3 points
(d) ten to twelve lessons—2 points
(e) more than twelve lessons—1 point
(f) not at all—0 points

### 7. After you teach your rat a trick, he:
(a) remembers the trick from then on—5 points
(b) occasionally needs some retraining—3 points
(c) seems to have a hard time remembering tricks—1 point

## SCORING

35 points—Your rat is very smart—a rattie genius!
24 to 34 points—Your rat is above average in intelligence.
19 to 23 points—Your rat is of average intelligence.
8 to 18—Your rat is below average in intelligence and could use some mental stimulation.
7 points or fewer—Your rat is a lovable little dummy.

[1] *Mysteries of Animal Intelligence: True Stories of Animals With Amazing Abilities*, by Sherry Hansen Steiger and Brad Steiger, published in 1995 by Tor Books (A Tom Doherty Associates Book). This book includes a one-page entry about a woman in New Jersey named Cindy Carroll who breeds rats and trained a rat to fetch.

# Resources

## CLUBS AND SOCIETIES

**American Fancy Rat and Mouse Association**
9230 64th Street
Riverside, CA 92509-5924
www.afrma.org

**National Fancy Rat Society**
PO Box 24207
London SE9 5ZF
www.nfrs.org

**Rat & Mouse Club of America**
6082 Modoc Road
Westminster, CA 92683
www.rmca.org

**Society of Michigan Rat Fanciers**
P.O. Box 610982
Port Huron, MI 48061-0982
www.michiganrats.org

**The Rat Fan Club**
Debbie "The Rat Lady" Ducommun
857 Lindo Lane
Chico CA 95973
(530) 899-0605
www.ratfanclub.org

## RESCUE AND ADOPTION ORGANIZATIONS

**Any Rat Rescue**
Glendale, AZ (Phoenix area)
602-595-0688
www.anyrat rescue.org

**Furry Friends Orphanage**
RMCA So. Cal.
Deborah Newgard
PO Box 4190
Costa Mesa, CA 92628
(949) 770-0323
ratzone1@aol.com

**Kim's Ark Rat Rescue**
www.kimsarkrescue.org
The largest rodent rescue on the East Coast.

**Rattie Ratz: Rescue, Resource, and Referral**
(Northern California)
2995 Woodside Road
Suite 400, PMB 325
Woodside, CA 94062
(650) 960-6994
www.rattieratz.com

**Small Animal Rescue Society of BC**
PO Box 54564
7155 Kingsway
Burnaby, BC V5E 4J6 Canada
Phone: 604-438-4366
Fax: 604-777-2118
www.smallanimalrescue.org

**Small Victories Rodent Rescue**
(514) 691-5263
http://mooshika.org/smallvictories/index.html
This group adopts out rescued rats and also lists other rats in Canada who need homes.

**Texas Rat Rescue**
http://www.heartoftexasrats.com/Rescue.htm

**The Best Little Rabbit, Rodent and Ferret House**
14317 Lake City Way NE
Seattle WA 98125
(206) 365-9105
www.rabbitrodentferret.org/rabbitrodentferret.org/index.asp

**Wee Companions Animal Adoption, Inc.**
San Diego, CA
(619) 934-6007
www.weecompanions.com

## Internet Resources
**The Agile Rat**
www.theagilerat.com
A comprehensive website on rat agility.

**Health Info and Veterinarian Referral List**
www.ratfanclub.org/helpinfo.html

**Northern Illinois Rat Organization**
www.niro-usa.org
NIRO is an organization dedicated to improving the rat fancy through careful and responsible breeding according to RSA standards, encouraging proper care and ownership, educating the public about the merits of rats as companion animals, and sharing ideas with others in order to broaden the collective knowledge of all fanciers.

**Rat Association of Texas**
http://ratassociation.org
An educational and social club in Texas.

**Rat Help**
http://wererat.net/rathelp/
Answers to frequently asked questions.

**RatsPacNW Rat Fanciers Club**
www.ratspacnw.org/
A Pacific Northwest rat club for breeders and fanciers.

**Rat Association of Texas**
http://ratassociation.org
An educational and social club in Texas.

**The Rat Fan Club**
Author's website.
www.ratfanclub.org

**World Rat Day**
http://www.worldratday.com
World Rat Day, a celebration of the rat, is April 4.

# PUBLICATIONS

## Magazines

*It's a Rat's World*
Borealis Arts, LLC
757 S. Kenyon Dr
Tucson, AZ 85710
(520) 790-1124
http://web.mac.com/itsaratsworld

*Pro-Rat-a*
National Fancy Rat Society
PO Box 24207
London SE9 5ZF
www.nfrs.org

*Rat & Mouse Tales*
American Fancy Rat and Mouse Association
9230 64th Street
Riverside, CA 92509-5924
www.afrma.org

*Rat-a-tat Chat*
Rat Assistance & Teaching Society
857 Lindo Lane
Chico, CA 95973
www.petrats.org

## Books

Ducommun, Debbie, *Rats: Practical, Accurate Advice from the Expert*, Bowtie Press.

Ducommun, Debbie, *Rat Health Care*, The Rat Fan Club.

Fox, Sue. *The Guide to Owning a Rat*. TFH Publications, Inc.

Hill, Lorraine. *Pet Owner's Guide to the Rat*, Interpet Publishing.

Page, Gill. *Getting to Know Your Rat*, Interpet Publishing.

# Index

# ABOUT THE AUTHOR

**Debbie Ducommun** has a B.A. degree in animal behavior and has worked in the animal care industry since 1977 in the areas of training, nutrition, and health care. She is the author of *Rats: Practical, Accurate Advice from the Expert.* She has also written a monthly column about small pets for *Pet Business* magazine since 1997 and has published 35 articles in other national magazines. In 1992, Debbie founded The Rat Fan Club to educate rat owners, and in 2003 founded the nonprofit organization Rat Assistance & Teaching Society (RATS) to educate pet-care professionals. Known as "The Rat Lady," Debbie is internationally recognized as an expert on domestic rats. She lives in Chico, CA, with her husband Larry and a varying number of rats.

# PHOTO CREDITS